EXPLAINING READING

SOLVING PROBLEMS IN THE TEACHING OF LITERACY
Cathy Collins Block, Series Editor

Recent Volumes

Best Practices in Adolescent Literacy Instruction
Edited by Kathleen A. Hinchman and Heather K. Sheridan-Thomas

Comprehension Assessment: A Classroom Guide
JoAnne Schudt Caldwell

Comprehension Instruction, Second Edition:
Research-Based Best Practices
Edited by Cathy Collins Block and Sheri R. Parris

The Literacy Coaching Challenge:
Models and Methods for Grades K–8
Michael C. McKenna and Sharon Walpole

Creating Robust Vocabulary:
Frequently Asked Questions and Extended Examples
Isabel L. Beck, Margaret G. McKeown, and Linda Kucan

Mindful of Words: Spelling and Vocabulary Explorations 4–8
Kathy Ganske

Finding the Right Texts:
What Works for Beginning and Struggling Readers
Edited by Elfrieda H. Hiebert and Misty Sailors

Fostering Comprehension in English Classes: Beyond the Basics
Raymond Philippot and Michael F. Graves

Language and Literacy Development: What Educators Need to Know
James P. Byrnes and Barbara A. Wasik

Independent Reading: Practical Strategies for Grades K–3
*Denise N. Morgan, Maryann Mraz, Nancy D. Padak,
and Timothy Rasinski*

Assessment for Reading Instruction, Second Edition
Michael C. McKenna and Katherine A. Dougherty Stahl

Literacy Growth for Every Child:
Differentiated Small-Group Instruction K–6
Diane Lapp, Douglas Fisher, and Thomas DeVere Wolsey

Explaining Reading, Second Edition: A Resource for Teaching
Concepts, Skills, and Strategies
Gerald G. Duffy

EXPLAINING READING

A Resource for Teaching Concepts, Skills, and Strategies

SECOND EDITION

Gerald G. Duffy

THE GUILFORD PRESS
New York   London

© 2009 The Guilford Press
A Division of Guilford Publications, Inc.
72 Spring Street, New York, NY 10012
www.guilford.com

Printed in the United States of America

This book is printed on acid-free paper.

Last digit is print number: 9 8 7 6 5 4 3 2 1

Library of Congress Cataloging-in-Publication Data
Duffy, Gerald G.
    Explaining reading : a resource for teaching concepts, skills, and
strategies / Gerald G. Duffy. — 2nd ed.
        p. cm. — (Solving problems in the teaching of literacy)
    ISBN 978-1-60623-075-6 (pbk.: alk. paper)
    ISBN 978-1-60623-076-3 (hardcover: alk. paper)
    1. Reading.   2. Reading—Remedial teaching.   3. Vocabulary.
I. Title.
    LB1050.42.D84 2009
    372.4—dc22

                                                                    2008050590

Teaching school well has always been difficult, but it is especially so now, when federal and state pressures, directives, and constraints threaten to deprofessionalize teaching. But I continue to be inspired by teachers who persist in being dedicated, thoughtful, and creative despite the difficulties. It is to them that this book is dedicated.

About the Author

Gerald G. Duffy, EdD, is the William Moran Distinguished Professor of Literacy and Reading at the University of North Carolina at Greensboro. Dr. Duffy spent 25 years teaching teachers how to teach reading and conducting research on classroom reading instruction at Michigan State University, where he was a Senior Researcher in the Institute for Research on Teaching and where he holds the rank of Professor Emeritus. He is also a former elementary and middle school teacher. A past President of the National Reading Conference and a member of the Reading Hall of Fame, Dr. Duffy has worked with teachers and children across the United States and overseas, has written and edited several books on reading instruction, and has published over 150 articles and research studies, with an emphasis on explicit teaching and teacher development.

Preface

This is the second edition of *Explaining Reading: A Resource for Teaching Concepts, Skills, and Strategies*. But my purpose is the same as it was for the first edition: to translate research on explicit teaching into a resource for busy teachers who, in the hurly-burly of day-to-day classroom life, often need a quick reference for how to help readers who do not "catch on" quickly.

Like the first edition, this edition emphasizes how to explain skills and strategies associated with vocabulary, comprehension, word recognition, and fluency to struggling readers. But this edition includes two major changes.

The first change reflects recent research on vocabulary and comprehension that has highlighted the importance of vocabulary development and the tension that exists between learning individual comprehension strategies and the ultimate goal of using families of strategies together. Consequently, Chapter 2, which describes vocabulary and comprehension, has been changed to reflect these findings, and the examples in Part II for explaining vocabulary and comprehension have been revised accordingly.

The second change is a heavier focus on the importance of teaching skills and strategies in meaningful contexts. This change has been driven by my work with teachers in the field who, almost universally, reported being pleased with the Part II examples but being frustrated about how to keep a focus on "real" reading. This was partly due to the times we live in, where the pressure is heavy to increase test scores, seemingly at the expense of developing children who *do* read. But I felt it might also be because the first edition, while including suggestions for how to ground instruction in real text, did not put enough emphasis on embedding explanations in authentic reading activity. Consequently, two additional changes in this new edition address that problem.

First, Chapter 1 emphasizes the need for "keeping the main thing the main thing" (i.e., teaching skills and strategies "inside" motivating reading tasks and activities). Specific ways teachers can accomplish this goal in busy classroom situations are described, and examples and reminders are also included in each Part II example.

Second, an entirely new Chapter 3 describes how to "explain the forest as well as the trees," with specific suggestions for doing so inserted into each of the Part II examples. The goal is to avoid perseverating on the nitty-gritty of skills and strategies (i.e., the trees) to the neglect of big understandings about why and how to use skills and strategies (i.e., the forest). When that happens, we run the risk that students will learn technical aspects of skills and strategies but will not learn to apply them when engaged in real reading.

In addition to the major changes in this edition, countless other clarifications, rewordings, and elaborations have been inserted throughout both the chapters and the Part II examples to improve clarity. Teachers often said the first edition was easy to read; I hope the second edition is even easier to read.

As with the first edition, it is important to make clear that the examples I provide in Part II are designed as "starters" to guide your thinking as you plan similar lessons. I provide them under the assumption that you will adapt and modify them to fit your classroom situation. For instance, while each example is rooted in authentic tasks that keep the focus on "the main thing," you will need to create your own "main thing" tasks using your own choice of text; while I use specific words to illustrate how a skill or strategy can be made explicit, you will need to use your own words; and while I describe many skills and strategies, you will need to assess before deciding whether a particular skill or strategy should be explained.

In sum, the four principles that defined the first edition continue to define the second. First, not all students need explicit explanations. Explanations are provided only when your assessment suggests that learning a specific skill or strategy would help. Second, deciding to explain does not mean abandoning efforts to "keep the main thing the main thing" by engaging students in useful and meaningful reading and writing tasks. Third, the examples provided here must be adapted and modified to fit your students' needs and your particular classroom situation. Finally, while the ultimate goal is for students to be "in the driver's seat," there are times when students need explicit help and the teacher must be in the driver's seat. This book is designed to be a resource when you are faced with such situations.

In short, to be successful in using this book, you must apply the suggestions I provide to the needs of your students. When preparing the first edition, I worried that teachers would use the book as a script, or would become too heavy-handed in providing explanations, or would fail to engage students in the instructional process. However, in my work with teachers in the field over the past 5 years, I have watched teacher after teacher use the Part II examples in thoughtful, creative, and student-centered ways. When that happens, this book can be very useful.

So, as with the first edition, it is my hope that the second edition will help you provide struggling readers with the skills and strategies they need to use text in enriching and empowering ways, and that you will find it to be a tool for making your instruction more adaptive, more differentiated, and more creative (as well as more explicit).

GERALD G. DUFFY

Contents

Examples for Explaining Comprehension Strategies

Examples for Explaining Word Recognition

Examples for Explaining Fluency

PART I

Background to Explaining

CHAPTER 1

The Foundation

KEEPING THE MAIN THING THE MAIN THING

There's an old saying: "The main thing is to keep the main thing the main thing." It applies directly to your use of this book.

This is a book about explaining reading skills and strategies. But explaining skills and strategies is *not* the main thing in teaching reading. The main thing is to inspire students to *be* readers.

If we teach skills and strategies, but our students do not become readers, we fail. So before discussing skills and strategies and how to explain them, I must first emphasize how to keep the main thing the main thing.

INSPIRING STUDENTS TO *BE* READERS

The main thing in reading is to develop students who *do* read. That means motivating them to read. But how do we do that?

We are helped to do it if we keep in mind an enduring teaching principle that says: "What they *do* is what they think it is." That is, what students *do* during "reading" time is what they think is the main thing about reading.

For instance, if during reading instruction students do skill sheets most of the time, they conclude that the main thing is doing isolated skills. But we want them to conclude that the main thing is to be readers. To accomplish that we must provide real reading tasks—tasks real readers do. For instance, when students spend much of their time using information in expository texts to accomplish a goal they set, they decide using reading to accomplish their goals is the main thing; if students read narratives about how people solve interpersonal problems similar to the ones students themselves are facing, they decide using reading to understand their world is the main thing. Other examples are:

- When real readers want to use a new video game, they read directions.
- When real readers want information about a matter of concern to them, they read expository text about the topic.
- When real readers are trying to decide about civic issues or current events, they read newspapers and magazines.
- When real readers want to pass the time in an entertaining way, they read popular novels.

The principle is that what students *do* during reading represents their experience with reading, and they use that experience to construct an understanding of why we read. So to motivate students to read, we must do two things: first, we ourselves must have a vision of what the main thing is in reading; second, we must create tasks or activities that give students experience doing the main thing.

What Does This Teacher Think Is the Main Thing?

In the second grade, Kendra was reading all the Laura Ingalls Wilder *Little House on the Prairie* books by herself. But her teacher noted that she didn't know what a schwa sound was. So she moved Kendra into the lowest reading group and told her to stop reading Laura Ingalls Wilder. Kendra had thought the main thing was independently reading and enjoying text. But what message is this teacher sending her?

In school, we often see "school reading," not "real reading." Typical school reading is artificial exercises such as completing worksheets.

We assign school reading because we think such practice is important, and students do those tasks because we tell them to. Similarly, we think it is sensible to have students read a story in a reading group and to answer questions about it, but this does not motivate some students because it is not what real readers do.

Real readers *do* something with what they read. So students think reading is important when they use reading to achieve a goal important to *them*, to achieve a purpose of *theirs*, or to answer questions *they* want answered. In short, they are motivated to read when reading empowers or enriches them.

The Game at the End of the Week

Many kids love to play baseball. They will practice skills such as fielding ground balls for hours without complaint. They are motivated to practice because there's a real game at the end of the week where they will *do* something important with those skills. What's "the game at the end of the week" in reading instruction? Are our students going to *do* something with the skills and strategies we teach?

As teachers, we believe it when we say "Reading is power." But for students to believe that reading is power, we must put them in position to experience the power of reading. That means they must *do* tasks and activities that demonstrate the power of reading.

HOW TEACHERS PROVIDE "REAL" READING

Classrooms are artificial places. Occasions for real reading are scarce. There are too many kids, too many things we are required to do, too many tests, too many directives from supervisors, and so on.

But despite such things, many teachers still manage to engage their kids in "real" reading. Four conditions make it possible: being committed to a vision of the main thing, having an organizational plan, setting realistic goals, and building a literate environment.

Being Committed to a Vision of the Main Thing

To provide students with real reading tasks and activities, we ourselves must have a vision for what we mean when we say "Reading is power." That is, we must have a vision for how we want our students to use reading in their lives. A vision is *your view* of what the main thing should be in reading instruction. Having a vision helps us decide what reading tasks our kids should engage in—that is, tasks that will give them experience with what it means when we say "Reading is power."

Examples of Teachers' Visions

Your vision brings literacy to life for students. Because you value what literacy can do for students in the real world, you strive to give students experiences with real-world reading. Some teachers envision reading as a means for being empowered, and plan experiences for students in which they read about ways to make the school playground safer or how to convince lawmakers to save the whales. Other teachers may envision reading as a vehicle for social improvement and may engage students in reading to decide how to improve services to the homeless or to help the elderly. Other teachers envision reading as a means for improving humanity and engage students in reading literature about the human condition. Still others envision reading as a practical tool and engage students in reading of application forms, driver's tests, newspapers, recipes, and reference materials.

It is difficult in an age of high-stakes testing to remain committed to a "main thing" vision. It often seems that, in the eyes of the public, the main thing is raising test scores. To sustain a main thing vision of reading as power, we must understand that, while we *do* want our students to score well on tests of skills and strategies, tests are only stepping stones toward the ultimate goal of *doing something* with what is read.

To communicate to our students that skills and strategies are just "stepping-stones" toward real reading, we must, as often as possible, provide experience with using reading as real readers do. Having a clear goal, or vision, is an important first step.

But while having a vision is important, it is not enough by itself. We also need to have an organizational plan, to be realistic, and to provide a supportive literate environment.

What's Wrong with the Following Reading Task?

In an attempt to involve her fifth graders in real reading, a teacher begins a unit on botany by telling her students that they are going to learn about plants so they can write a persuasive article about why plants are important. But the kids don't get motivated. Why? Probably because writing a persuasive article was the teacher's choice, not the students' choice, and because their persuasive articles were not going to be used to persuade anyone. If, on the other hand, the kids had had a voice in deciding to write the articles, and if they had known they were going to send them to someone who really needed to be persuaded, it is more likely the kids would have been motivated.

An Organizational Plan

It is not easy to provide students with experiences in real reading. It requires that we teach skills and strategies *inside* larger tasks or activities. That is, we first engage students in real reading tasks— and then, within those larger tasks, teach the skills and strategies needed to accomplish the goal or complete the task.

An Example of Teaching a Strategy Inside a Larger Task

Consider the following example of a third-grade teacher. She must teach her students what an index is and how to use it. She could just provide an explicit explanation of how to use an index and then give them a worksheet for practice. But she does not do that because her vision is that her students will experience reading as empowering. Consequently, because she knows her students are concerned that new animal control laws passed by the township might result in the cruel treatment of cats, she invites her students to influence how the town council enforces the new laws. The students read for information they can use to convince the town council. So they experience what it means when we say "Reading is power"—because through their reading they can see that they will impact their world. But in the midst of that reading—that is, *inside* that larger activity—the teacher provides explicit instruction in how to use an index to find the information they need to solve the problem. So by first involving students in real reading tasks, this teacher accomplishes two goals: she motivates students by engaging them in what real readers do and she provides explicit instruction on how to use an index to accomplish the task.

The organizational plan, then, is to look for opportunities for students to experience real reading tasks. When those opportunities arise, use them as the basic activity or task. Then, within that activity, teach necessary skills or strategies.

Being Realistic

Most of us are not creative enough to transform the classroom into a place where every reading activity is an authentic reading task. And because practice exercises, tests, and school-like tasks are a necessary part of learning to read, we do not want to eliminate them totally. So we must choose our spots. We look for occasional opportunities, and when they arise, we make a big deal out of the fact that this is what reading is really all about.

Here are several hints about how to think about opportunities for "real reading."

- Utilize the content areas of social studies, science, and health for real reading opportunities; they provide more practical applications.
- Integrate reading and writing into a content area; doing so is time-efficient but, more important, doing so illustrates how reading and writing are useful tools.
- Initiate week-long or month-long themes or units that give you time for real reading and for explicitly teaching skills and strategies *inside* the real reading task.
- Ensure that themes or units have a culminating activity or a tangible product or some other obvious conclusion that stu-

dents see as important; this gives students a clear goal to work toward and gives you a chance to say, "See how reading helped you get what you wanted to get?"

In short, we are not always able to transform school reading into real reading. The important thing is that we try to do so as often as possible. So if you cannot create genuine reading tasks every day, you are typical. However, you should as often as possible engage students in activity that gives them experience with why reading is important.

The Power of Expectancy

Setting a positive expectancy is a powerful teacher tool. *Expecting* students to do real reading becomes a "self-fulfilling prophecy." That is, immersing students in real reading often inspires them to rise to your expectation and to develop their own visions for reading. In short, they are motivated by your passion for using reading for authentic purposes.

Building a Supportive Literate Environment

A literate classroom is designed to provide real reading and writing. To some extent, it is a state of mind because the environment you design for your classroom reflects your vision for what you think the main thing is in reading. Consequently, literate environments may differ from classroom to classroom depending on a teacher's vision.

However, six conditions are present in one form or another in all literate environments. These conditions are important because they send students messages about important aspects of reading.

1. *Fill the class environment with text.* If exciting and interesting texts are available in the classroom, students are more likely to be enticed to read. Consequently, students should have access to a wide range of high-quality trade books, both narrative and expository. The usual guideline is at least 30 trade books per student, including a wide range of genres and levels of difficulty attractively arranged to encourage browsing. There might be beanbag chairs or rocking chairs

in an area where trade books are displayed on racks with the covers out. Daily read-alouds of good books are also important. Additionally there should be lots of non-book texts, including maps, globes, student-generated text, charts the teachers and students produce and display in the classroom, and magazines and newspapers. And, of course, students should have access to computers, both for generating text through word processing and for accessing information via the Internet.

2. *Organize the classroom so that students have lots of time to read.* The general guideline is that students should do 45–60 minutes of easy reading every school day. The time can be broken up, with 15 minutes during a designated free reading time, 7 minutes during a break in activities, and so on. But students do not learn to read unless they read a lot. And they cannot get better by reading difficult material. This is especially so for struggling readers.

Focus on Connected Text

Students should read and write "connected text." *Connected text* is text that contains a coherent message. A story is an example of connected text; a chapter in a social studies book is connected text; a newspaper article is connected text. Fill-in-the-blank worksheets or word lists are *not* connected texts. While we may want students to fill in blanks or work with isolated words on occasion, students become readers by reading connected text.

---

3. *Build rich oral and written vocabulary.* Reading is language, and language is made up of words. Words reflect experiences. For instance, you know what "piedmont" means if you have experienced living in North Carolina or if you have done a lot of reading and talking about the Piedmont region of the United States. The more experiences you have, the more words you have; and the more words you have, the more likely it is that you will become a good reader. Because new words come from new experiences, literate classroom environments are characterized by rich experiences with content areas such as science and social studies. These translate into new vocabulary. The richer the vocabulary, the more likely it is that students will become readers.

4. *Make writing an integral part of the classroom context.* Writing and reading are mutually supportive. The more students read, the better they write; the more they write, the better they read. Consequently, writing should be prevalent in the classroom. The guideline here is that students should write at least 30 minutes a day. Again, the emphasis should be on connected text. Writing to complete worksheets or to do spelling tests may occasionally be necessary, but the writing of connected text is what develops literacy. Examples include writing in journals, writing stories, writing letters, writing notes to friends or family, writing expository text in support of a class project, and so on.

5. *Include multiple opportunities for students to read under your guidance.* You should allocate some instructional time to guiding students through selections in basal textbooks, literature selections, and content-area texts such as social studies, science, and mathematics. Such instructional experiences are opportunities for you to reinforce important learning and to engage students in rich language experiences while also providing a social occasion for sharing together.

6. *Emphasize conversational talk in the classroom.* In a supportive literate environment, you and your students discuss topics together. Avoid traditional question-and-answer formats as much as possible. Instead, give students a voice. Their role in classroom talk should be more collaborative than submissive, more active than passive, more conversational than interrogative.

SUMMARY

In sum, skills and strategies must be explained within a larger context: a classroom environment designed to communicate to students the main thing about reading. Explaining occurs, but because it occurs *inside* real reading tasks, students build the understanding that reading is useful. Each of the examples in Part II of this book includes a suggested way to keep the main thing the main thing.

Keeping the main thing the main thing is crucial for two reasons.

First, it helps you. In emphasizing the main thing, you state a personal value, saying, in effect, "I teach because I'm creating something important in my classroom. What you see my students doing here in my classroom is my vision for what I want them to value about reading."

Second, it helps students. Students decide what reading is and develop their own ideas about why it is worth learning on the basis of their experiences. If a class environment causes them to experience reading as important and personally rewarding, they are more likely to become readers; if they experience reading as boring or dumb or unfulfilling, all the explaining in the world may not make them into readers.

In sum, reading instruction tends to be more successful when it is organized around important tasks you and your students pursue together. The nitty-gritty of learning skills and strategies happens *inside* those tasks. Students get two important psychological boosts as a result. First, they are inspired by your passion for "reading as power." Second, because the classroom tasks are indeed genuine forms of taking action and not just boring "school stuff," students are motivated. From these twin forces, students develop the belief that reading and writing is important, and they persist in the face of difficulties.

CHAPTER 2

Skills and Strategies
to Be Learned

Within the main thing, as described in Chapter 1, three important categories of skills and strategies are important when learning to read:

1. Vocabulary and comprehension strategies.
2. Skills and strategies for identifying (or decoding) words.
3. Skills and strategies for how to read fluently.

This chapter describes each of these three categories in a general way. Specific examples of how to explain each skill and strategy are provided in Part II.

Skill or Strategy?

What is a skill and what is a strategy? A *skill* is something you do automatically without thinking about it. You do it the same way every time. Tying your shoes is an example of a skill. An example of a reading skill is instantly recognizing and saying a word such as *the*. You do these things without thinking about them. They are automatized. A *strategy*, in contrast, is a plan. You reason when you do it, and you often adjust the plan as you go along. When you plan a trip by car, you are thoughtful, making decisions about what highways to take, where to spend the night, and so on. And if you run

---

into unanticipated problems along the way (such as extensive road construction), you adjust your strategy—you change your route. In reading, making predictions is a strategy because readers are thoughtful in using text clues and prior knowledge to make an initial prediction, but they remain ready to change or adjust a prediction when subsequent text clues provide more information.

VOCABULARY AND COMPREHENSION

This section focuses on vocabulary and comprehension. Comprehension is the essence of reading because the goal of written language is communication of messages. If we do not understand the message, we are not reading. And vocabulary is fundamentally important for understanding the message.

When Should We Start Teaching Vocabulary and Comprehension?

It is often assumed that vocabulary and comprehension should be delayed until after students have learned how to decode. Not so. Vocabulary and comprehension instruction can be started as early as preschool if we use listening situations. Comprehending oral messages requires the same strategies as comprehending printed messages, so the earlier we start emphasizing vocabulary and comprehension the more likely it is that students will see it as a priority.

Vocabulary: A Basis of Good Comprehension

Reading comprehension depends on prior knowledge or knowledge about the world. Prior knowledge is expressed with words. When comprehending, readers say to themselves, in effect, "In my experience with words associated with this topic or situation, the author must mean something close to what I've experienced." So they use the words in the text to build a meaning consistent with their past experience with these words.

When the meaning of a word is unknown, it means the reader does not have background knowledge or has not had experiences in that area. Without background knowledge—that is, without the vocabulary that comes with various experiences—there is no comprehension.

How Vocabulary and Prior Knowledge Are Related

As schoolteachers, most of us would have difficulty comprehending a text on nuclear reactors. We do not have much prior knowledge about nuclear reactors, so we do not know the meaning of the words used to describe nuclear reactors. Physicists, in contrast, know those words, and can construct subtle and complex meaning. Similarly, children who have always lived in New York City have little prior knowledge about buttes and mesas—that is, they do not have meaning for those words—so they would have more difficulty constructing meaning for a text about the desert southwest; in contrast, children from Phoenix would find it easier because they have experienced "buttes" and "mesas" and therefore know what those words mean.

In short, you cannot construct a meaning unless you have experiences with the word meanings associated with a topic. So vocabulary instruction is crucial.

"Natural" Vocabulary Development versus Direct Teaching

The best way to increase vocabulary is by immersing students in written and oral language, both in the home and in the literate environment of the classroom. Given a rich language background at home, immersion in substantive subject-matter knowledge in school, and lots of experiences with new concepts and ideas, vocabulary often develops "naturally" with no intentional instruction. But when those conditions are not present, some students do not develop adequate vocabularies. In those cases, teachers must provide more direct vocabulary instruction in order to develop students' vocabularies sufficiently.

New words can be learned through direct experience, as when new words about farms and farm animals are encountered on a field trip to a real farm, or they can be learned through vicarious experience, as when one reads new words about farms and farm animals or hears them used in a video or on TV. In school, most new word meanings are learned vicariously.

Students should learn at least 1,000–2,000 new vocabulary words each school year to become highly literate. The traditional way to develop vocabulary is by providing definitions, often through dictionary work. However, this has limited effect. Students may memorize a word and its definition, but they almost always forget it.

A much better plan is to intentionally and directly teach the meanings of 10–15 new words students will read and use each week. Normally, it is best to draw the 10–15 new words from content areas such as social studies and science because those areas involve new information students have not previously experienced.

How Important Is Prior Knowledge?

It has been estimated that as much as 50–60% of successful comprehension is tied to background knowledge. Knowing something about a topic before one begins to read—that is, knowing the meaning of the words used—is crucial to being able to construct meaning from a text.

In addition to intentionally and directly teaching 10–15 new words weekly, we should also teach strategies students can use to figure out word meanings they encounter when reading independently. Many of the new words students learn are encountered during independent reading. By teaching strategies for figuring out unknown words as you read, students can learn more than just the 10–15 weekly words. The two major strategies for figuring out words independently are context and structural (or morphemic) analysis.

Part II of this book provides four examples you can use to guide your teaching of vocabulary. The first two are examples of how to intentionally and directly teach word meanings: one shows how you might explain how word meaning is tied to critical attributes and distinguishing features (see Example 1); the other shows how to use semantic maps to build categories for words (see Example 2). The next two are examples of strategies for figuring out a word meaning when reading independently: the first is an example of how to explain the use of context as a strategy to figure out word meaning independently (see Example 3); the second is an example of how to explain the use of structural analysis as a strategy to figure out word meaning independently (see Example 4).

How Comprehension Works

Comprehension is strategic. If we have prior knowledge about a topic in a text, we can use strategies—or plans—to construct meaning based on our experience, and we can adjust and change those plans as we go along. The box below illustrates some of the distinguishing characteristics of comprehension. I have tried to demonstrate that comprehension is a continuous process of using text clues—mainly word meanings but also syntactic clues—to access relevant categories of prior knowledge and, on the basis of our own experience with those categories of knowledge, making predictions about what meaning is to come. Typically, subsequent text clues cause us to access different categories of knowledge and to either abandon or adjust a first prediction in favor of a new or modified prediction that fits the new information. It is a fluid cycle of trial and error in which a reader uses prior knowledge to predict what meaning is coming, monitors during reading to see what does come next, revises the prediction when an anticipated meaning does not pan out, problem-solves when blockages to meaning occur, and reflects on what has been read after finishing reading.

An Example of How Comprehension Works

To illustrate the way comprehension works, let's try to comprehend a bit of text, piece by piece. We look first at the title. It says "The Unanticipated Destination." As soon as we see that, our minds begin to generate hypotheses, or predictions. We begin to activate our own experiences about trips and about starting out to go to one place but then ending up in another. Assuming we all have similar background experiences, we anticipate that this is a story about a trip, and we get ready for that meaning.

Then we look at the first line of the selection. It says, "I flew into GEG." Several things happen at once. You look at the word "flew" and access the "flying" category in your mind. While you may have originally been thinking of a trip by car, you now dump that image and replace it with an image of airplanes (again, if your background experiences are different, you might generate a different image). If you have experience flying commercially, you probably think about a large jet airplane, and you see an image in your mind of rows of people sitting in the coach section (teachers seldom create an image of the first-class section since few of us have had experience sitting in first class). If you have never flown, however, your image of what it looks like on the inside of an airplane will be limited to what you have experienced in movies or in magazines and, as such, will probably be less detailed. And while you may use the syntactic clue "into" to figure out that "GEG" must be a place, you will probably be mystified as to exactly what that place is (unless, of course, you fly a lot and have lots of experience finding your baggage, in which case you have already figured out that GEG is an airport identifier, and that GEG is an airport). You may even know that GEG is the Spokane, Washington, airport if your experiences include travel to the northwest.

Now let's look at the next line of the selection. It says, "But they wouldn't let me land." If up until now we had pictured people sitting in the coach section of a large jet airplane, that image is now replaced by the image of a pilot in the cockpit of an airplane. Our experience tells us that if the passenger image had been correct, the sentence would have said, "But they wouldn't let *us* land." It is only the pilot who says "They wouldn't let *me* land." So we change our prediction. We begin thinking about pilots, not passengers.

So, we say comprehension is:

- Proactive, because a reader must be actively thinking and constantly monitoring the meaning.
- Tentative, because predictions made in one moment may change in the next moment.
- Personal, in that meaning resides in the reader's interpretation, which in turn is controlled by his or her prior knowledge.
- Transactive, because the reader's background interacts with the author's intention.
- Thoughtful, because you must always analyze the clues the author provides.
- Imagistic, because (in narrative text particularly) you use the author's descriptive language to create a picture in your mind of what is happening.

- Inferential, because the reader can only make a calculated guess about the author's meaning since the author was operating from one set of experiences and the reader from another.
- Reflective, in that good readers evaluate what they have read and determine its significance and/or how it can be used after finishing reading.

Strategies are an important part of comprehension. There are only a few strategies readers use in various combinations over and over again, with slight variation from one reading situation to another. These include:

- Making predictions.
- Monitoring and questioning what is happening.
- Adjusting predictions as you go.
- Creating images in the mind.
- Removing blockages to meaning.
- Reflecting on the essence or the significance or the importance of what has been read.

These strategies can be categorized as:

- Before you begin reading.
- As you begin reading.
- During reading.
- After reading.

Avoiding Rigidity

Describing comprehension strategies as "before," "as you begin," "during," and "after" is a helpful organizational structure for students because it emphasizes the ongoing continuous pursuit of meaning from before starting to read until well after the last page has been turned. However, the categories are not rigid. Strategies used primarily as you begin may also be used throughout; strategies listed as after strategies can (and often should) be used throughout. Students should be made aware of this, as well as of the fact that, ultimately, strategies are combined and used together, not separately.

Before-You-Begin Strategies

Readers are more motivated, and comprehend more, when they are reading for a purpose that makes sense to them. So the best reading experiences begin with the reader asking, "Why am I reading this?" "How will I use it?" Even if the text is a story being read just for enjoyment, the purpose should be clear to the reader.

This again takes us back to Chapter 1 and the importance of keeping the main thing the main thing. By starting any reading experience with a clear purpose for reading, we are more likely to develop students who *do* read.

As-You-Begin Strategies

Predicting is the strategy relied upon most as you begin. As soon as a reader sees the title of a selection or looks at a picture on a cover or reads a first line, prior knowledge is triggered and, on the basis of that prior knowledge, predictions (or hypotheses) are formed about what is to come. Predictions can be based on three kinds of prior knowledge.

1. *Prior knowledge about the purpose of the reading.* As noted above, a crucial before-you-read question is, "Why am I reading this?" It is crucial because having a viable reason for reading is key to motivation. But purpose also can suggest what one looks for when reading, or what predictions to make. For instance, when reading the morning paper, a reader may be concerned with the gist of a news article but not the details, and will seek only the gist. In contrast, when reading a recipe, predictions focus on details because details are crucial to cooking tasks.

2. *Prior knowledge about the topic.* Topic is also important as you begin. For instance, if a reader picks up a book with a picture of an elephant on the cover, or if one of the first sentences is about elephants, it is anticipated that something will be learned about elephants, and the reader uses what is known about elephants to make predictions about what is coming.

3. *Prior knowledge about type of text.* The type of text directs readers as they begin. Recognizing the text as a narrative, for examples, triggers prior knowledge about story structure, and we expect we will learn about a setting, a character, and a problem in the first

few pages. Recognizing a text as expository, in contrast, triggers prior knowledge about fact books and information.

See Example 5 in Part II for guidance on explaining how to predict.

During-Reading Strategies

The primary strategy used during reading is a combination of monitoring, questioning, and repredicting (see Example 6). Successful readers pay attention to what is happening and anticipate that there might be a need to change a prediction. It is as if readers are constantly engaged in silent questioning, saying to themselves as they read along, "Does this make sense? Does this make sense? Does this make sense?" When a reader answers by saying, "No, this no longer makes sense," then a new prediction must be made.

The predicting, monitoring, and repredicting cycle is repeated over and over again as the reader proceeds through text. It is not a static, one-time process. It is a process that goes on constantly. As readers become proficient, strategies in this cycle are no longer individual entities. They are combined together so that the process seems to be one big strategy.

While the predicting–monitoring–repredicting cycle is the dominant during-reading strategy, other strategies are also sometimes used. For instance, in narrative text with descriptive language, good comprehenders may use their prior knowledge to create images—that is, to infer what the scene in the narrative looks like or feels like (see Example 7). Similarly, when the need arises, successful readers stop and use fix-it strategies to problem-solve a blockage to meaning (see Example 9). In such cases, good readers say to themselves, "What is the problem that has stopped me here?" and "What strategies have I learned that I could use to fix this problem?"

- Sometimes the problem is a word having an unknown meaning, whereupon the reader might apply a context clue strategy to figure out the meaning.
- Sometimes the problem involves syntactic (or word-order) elements, whereupon the reader might do a "look-back" in which the material is read again.

- Sometimes the problem is a lack of a meaningful connection, whereupon the reader will search for relevant prior knowledge from past experience.
- Sometimes the problem is a lost focus for why the material is being read in the first place, whereupon the reader will stop and rethink how the reading is to be used.

Comprehension Requires Making Inferences

Inferring (or "reading between the lines") is often taught as a separate strategy (see Example 8). In fact, however, all reading comprehension requires the reader to make inferences. When a reader makes a prediction, he or she uses background knowledge to "infer" what will come next. We call it "predicting" but predicting is an inference. Even answering a literal question requires inferring (if a text says "The girl wore her "best dress," the reader infers, based on his or her personal experience, what a best dress looks like). Because comprehenders are always using text cues and background knowledge to construct meaning, they are always reading between the lines or making inferences about what the author intends.

In sum, the most important during-reading strategy is the predict–monitor–repredict cycle. In certain situations, readers will use a fix-it strategy, but often the "fix" occurs in the process of predicting–monitoring–repredicting. Similarly, some narrative texts will require students to use descriptive language to infer an image, but it too is often embedded in the process of predicting–monitoring–repredicting. As noted earlier, comprehension involves use of relatively few strategies in various combinations. A good example is the way good comprehenders combine predicting–monitoring–repredicting during reading.

After-Reading Strategies

Comprehension does not stop when the last page of a selection is read. Good readers reflect after they read. They ask themselves questions such as:

- Did I achieve the purpose I had for reading this selection?
- Did I find out what I wanted to find out?

- How has my thinking changed as a result of the reading I just did?
- Is what I found out important or accurate?
- How can I use what I read?

The following are important after-reading strategies:

- Deciding on the text's important message or main idea (see Example 10).
- Determining theme (see Example 11).
- Summarizing (see Example 12).
- Drawing conclusions (see Example 13).
- Evaluating (see Example 14).
- Synthesizing (see Example 15).

The Importance of Combining Strategies

Even though we organize comprehension into "before," "as you begin," "during," and "after"-strategies, good readers often combine them and use them throughout the reading process. For instance, during reading a good reader may decide on the main idea and make evaluative judgments and otherwise employ "after" reading strategies. The important thing about presenting comprehension as before, as you begin, during, and after is that it communicates the big understanding that comprehension is a continuous process and that thinking continues after the last page of text has been read.

Summarizing Comprehension

Comprehension is difficult to teach because the process is fluid. We cannot proceduralize comprehension or teach comprehension "rules" because:

1. Different readers have different background experiences and construct different meanings.
2. Readers must adapt comprehension strategies to many different kinds of text situations.
3. Successful readers seldom implement each strategy separately but instead combine several strategies together.

How All Comprehension Strategies Are Alike

While it is difficult to teach comprehension, there is one thing we can count on. All comprehension strategies require readers to access and apply background knowledge. In this sense, comprehension is a single strategy—that of applying your experience to construct meaning. The heart of being "a strategic reader," therefore, is the understanding that all individual strategies are more alike than different. That is, all comprehension strategies require readers to examine the text cue, access background knowledge about that cue, make an inference about the meaning based on one's experience, and then monitoring and repredicting if necessary. In short, the thinking process is basically the same to predict, to infer, to create images, to figure out the main idea, and so on. What changes is the complexity of the text and the purpose for reading.

WORD RECOGNITION

Word recognition is decoding the printed squiggles on the page. There are two major ways readers decode words:

1. They instantly identify many words at sight.
2. When a word is not recognized instantly, they analyze the word to figure out what it is.

Sight Word Recognition

You cannot read smoothly and fluently, in oral or silent reading, if you cannot quickly say the words.

Learning sight words is a visual memory task. Good readers memorize words once they have seen them a few times.

Without a large stock of sight words, reading becomes a laborious, slow, and boring task of figuring out word after word.

Sight Recognition versus Phonics

Sight word recognition should not be confused with phonics. Knowing a word at sight means remembering the word's visual form as a whole. The recognition is instant. There is no "figuring out" involved. Phonics, in contrast, is figuring out by sounding out words letter by letter. While sight word recognition is fast, phonics is slow.

Preparing to Learn Sight Words

Most children come to school with little in their background that prepares them for print detail. For a 5-year-old, the relatively minor differences between a *d* and a *b* or between an *m* and an *n* just do not seem important. But being able to note tiny visual differences in print detail is an important prerequisite to sight word acquisition.

Learning to attend to print detail is sometimes called "visual discrimination" (see Example 16). The trick in visually differentiating among letters and words is to note the *differences* in the visual forms.

Lots of children develop visual discrimination skills almost naturally as a result of early writing experiences. But sometimes writing is not enough. Often, we need to be explicit about explaining what makes a *u* different from an *n* or what distinguishes *was* from *saw*.

Look-Alike Words

Failure to learn to discriminate among print forms often shows up later as a deterrent to fluency. For instance, when students routinely say "want" for "went," or "then" for "when," or "where" for "there," or confuse any number of other look-alike words, it is very difficult for them to become smooth, fluent readers. These confusions are often rooted in not examining the print forms carefully enough to note what discriminates one from the other. While good users of context will often go back and correct such miscues, such "lookbacks" can, if they occur too often, slow the reader down.

Learning Sight Words

Sight word recognition is the skill of remembering words. Again, little in the backgrounds of some 5-year-olds prepares them for holding visual forms of words in their memories. They may remember the

M in McDonald's, their name, and words such as *dinosaur* and *elephant* because those words have strong meaning for them. But high-utility words in the English language that serve important grammatical functions, such as *the, into,* and *with* are often much more difficult.

Good adult readers recognize at sight virtually every word they encounter. They accomplish this primarily by doing lots and lots of reading of connected text. The more they read, the more words they encounter; the more words they encounter, the more words they remember and recognize instantly. So, one way to develop sight words is to ensure that your students do a lot of reading of easy connected text.

However, sometimes students also need explicit instruction in how to remember sight words. Example 17 in Part II provides an example you can use to plan your own explanations of how to remember a word as a sight word.

The most common and highly utilized words in the English language are taught first. That is, because *the* appears so often, we teach it as a sight word almost immediately. Similarly, we emphasize the other crucial "glue" words that appear so frequently in English.

Words that cannot be figured out using phonics are also taught as sight words. For instance, words like *come* and *comb* do not follow standard rules of phonics and are taught as sight words.

Gradually, however, virtually all words become sight words. In third-grade social studies, for instance, readers may encounter the word *geography* for the first time. On that first occasion, they may have to slowly figure out what the word is or have the teacher identify it. Similarly, they may have to slowly figure it out the second time they encounter it, and the third time. But by the fourth or fifth time they see *geography*, they should no longer be figuring it out. They just say it, because it has now become a sight word.

Analyzing Words

Word analysis is what a reader does when a word is not recognized at sight and it must be figured out.

There are three major analysis techniques: (1) phonics, (2) context, and (3) structural analysis. Good readers will use all three techniques in combination.

Analyzing Words Using Phonics

Phonics is using alphabet letters and their sounds to figure out unknown words.

How often should a reader have to sound out a word? If a child is given appropriate reading material, only a limited number of words are not known at sight. A good rule of thumb for narrative text is that at least 90–95% of the words on a page should be recognized at sight in order for a student to read the text without becoming frustrated and discouraged. That means that no more than 5% or 10% of the words on the page would need to be sounded out. So, phonics is applicable only 5% or 10% of the time. It is "for emergency use only."

An Exception to the 90–95% Rule

When students read expository text, more than 10% of the words may be unknown to them. In such cases, they should not be expected to read the text unassisted. Instead, teachers should provide support in the form of vocabulary assistance, study guides, guided reading, and other aids.

Phonics instruction consists of three major components: (1) phonemic awareness, (2) letter–sound associations, and (3) decoding by analogy.

PHONEMIC AWARENESS

Phonemic awareness is the ability to hear and discriminate sounds in the mind (see Example 18).

Phonemic awareness is not phonics; it is a prerequisite to phonics. Students will have great difficulty with phonics (i.e., with associating letters with their sounds) if they cannot first discriminate one sound from another. Consequently, phonemic awareness is a "sound-only" skill. Letter names are not used.

Types of Phonemic Awareness

Phonemic awareness is the ability to distinguish sounds we hear. Beginning readers need to be able to identify rhyming words and discriminate beginning and ending sounds of words. For instance, if I say "cat" and "rat," can you tell me if they begin the same or differently? Do they end the same or differently?

Students should also be able to segment sounds in words or to stretch out the sounds in a word. For instance, if I say the word *man*, can you discriminate the individual sounds in the word and say them "stretched out," as in "*m-m-a-a-a-n-n*"?

And students should be able to blend sounds or put sounds back together. For instance, if I say "*m-m-a-a-a-n-n*" can you tell me that the word I'm saying is *man*?

Many children come to school already possessing highly refined phonemic awareness skills. They have played word games at home, and have sung songs, and have listened to poems and stories that have funny sounds in them. When children have such experiences at home, they come to school with the ability to discriminate one sound from another and to manipulate those sounds in their minds. Those children are then ready to learn phonics.

However, not all children have played with sounds. Some come to school without being able to discriminate one sound from another. These children need phonemic awareness training.

LETTER–SOUND ASSOCIATIONS

Once children can discriminate among sounds in their mind, they are ready to learn what sound goes with what letter (see Example 19).

Letter–sound association can be very complicated because there are lots of letter sounds in the English language. Vowels and vowel combinations are particularly difficult because one vowel letter can make different sounds in different words. Consequently, beginning phonics instruction emphasizes the most utilitarian sounds: the consonants.

Consonants are the most useful and stable of phonic sounds. They are often the beginning and ending letters in words, and they have relatively few sound variations.

Consequently, initial phonics instruction emphasizes:

- Single-consonant sounds.
- Consonant blends (in which two or more consonants are blended together, as in the *bl* in *blend* and the *dr* in *draw*).

- Consonant digraphs (in which two consonants together make a new consonant sound, as in the *sh* in *ship* and the *th* in *think*).

Traditionally, phonics instruction has also emphasized the teaching of vowel sounds, but it is a laborious task, and success is often limited. Recently there has been a shift away from teaching individual vowel sounds in favor of "decoding by analogy."

Decoding by Analogy

Decoding by analogy is a strategy in which a reader uses known spelling patterns to figure out unknown words having the same pattern (see Example 20). It is the most efficient way to teach vowel sounds.

Many words are made up of consonants combined with common phonograms containing a vowel or vowels (recently the consonant has been called the "onset" and the vowel pattern or phonogram has been called the "rime"). For instance, the word *cat* consists of the initial consonant (or onset) of *c* and the phonogram (or rime) of *-at*. When we know a word like *cat*, we can figure out other words having the same spelling pattern (or vowel sound), such as *sat, rat, bat,* and *flat*.

Decoding by analogy can also be used to figure out multisyllable words. For instance, a long word such as *envelope* can be figured out if the student knows a word having the common spelling pattern *-en* (such as *then*) and another having the pattern *-ell* (such as *tell*) and another having the pattern *-ope* (such as *hope*).

It calls for a reader to create an analogy from a known word to an unknown word. It is a strategy because it must be applied thoughtfully, not automatically or unconsciously.

Using Word Walls

There are two kinds of word walls. One is an alphabetic word wall. It lists alphabetically words students are expected to spell correctly. If they do not remember how to spell the word but they know the first letter, they can look at the word wall to determine the correct spelling.

A second kind of word wall—and the one most relevant here— is used to help students decode by analogy. When a word having a common spelling pattern is encountered in reading, it is identified and learned as a sight word. This sight word is then put on the word wall, and words with the same spelling pattern are listed under it. When students encounter unknown words in their reading, they look for words on the word wall that have the same spelling pattern as the unknown word. Then they can use the spelling pattern in the word on the word wall to figure out by analogy how to say the unknown word they encountered in their reading.

Analyzing Words Using Context

Context is a technique in which the meaning around an unknown word is used to make a calculated prediction about what the unknown word could be.

If, for instance, a reader encounters the unknown word *umbrella* in the sentence "It was raining, so I put up my _____," it is not necessary to go through the longer process of sounding out the word. Given the structure of the sentence and prior experience with umbrellas, it is obvious what the unknown word is.

Context is a strategy because the reader must be thoughtful and use prior knowledge to decide what the unknown word is. It is often the preferred way of figuring out an unknown word, because it is faster and more efficient than sounding out, especially when context and phonics are used together (see Example 21). For instance, context provides limited help in the sentence "It was raining, so I put *on* my _____." But if we add a phonic cue, such as the letter *h* in the initial position in the blank, we can be more likely to predict the unknown word.

Even beginning readers should be taught to use context. For instance, when kindergartners listen to stories being read to them by their teacher, they can learn to use the meaning to predict orally what word would fill a particular spot in the text. When students are given lots of experience in listening for and using context clues during pre-reading listening activities, they find it easier to use the same process in reading later on.

Analyzing Words Using Structural Analysis

Structural analysis uses word parts such as root words, prefixes, suffixes, inflectional endings, and Greek and Latin roots to identify unrecognized words. Linguists call these word parts "morphemes," so structural analysis is sometimes referred to as "morphemic analysis." Because morphemes have meaning, structural analysis can also be used as a strategy for figuring out *the meaning* of a word (see Example 4).

To illustrate how it works for identifying unrecognized words, consider an unknown word such as *unhappy*. We can separate the root *happy* from the prefix *un* and then say the word. Similarly, an unknown word such as *flying* can be figured out by separating the root *fly* from the inflectional ending *ing*.

Structural analysis is not as utilitarian as phonics or context because not all unknown words contain prefixes, suffixes, inflectional endings, or Greek and Latin roots.

Example 4, on using structural analysis to figure out word meaning, can be adapted and used when planning explanations of structural analysis for word analysis purposes.

Summarizing Word Recognition

Several misconceptions about word recognition instruction deserve emphasis:

- First, word recognition is not taught first and comprehension later. Comprehension and word recognition are both taught from the start.
- Second, word recognition is not just about phonics. To the contrary, what distinguishes fluent, motivated readers is their ability to recognize lots of words at sight. Phonics is an analysis technique. It should be used only when a reader encounters an unrecognized word. And if the reader is placed in appropriate material, there should be only a few unrecognized words per hundred words encountered.
- Finally, the ultimate goal in word recognition instruction is that readers recognize virtually all words at sight, with unknown

words figured out using a combination of context, phonics, and (if there are structural units present) structural analysis.

FLUENCY

Fluency is the ability to orally and silently read text smoothly and with appropriate phrasing and intonation. We often refer to it as "reading like you talk." Fluency is often thought to be limited to oral reading. While this is the case with emergent readers, the real fluency issue is how to help students become fluent *silent* readers. Reading like you talk, therefore, is descriptive of silent reading for postbeginning readers.

Being fluent in both oral and silent reading is a function of:

1. How fast or slow one reads.
2. Whether the phrasing and intonation accurately reflects the meaning in the text.

Fluency is often determined by noting a reader's reading rate (words read per minute). However, the number of words read per minute does not take into account correct phrasing and intonation. To be an accurate measure of fluency, assessment should include not only speed but also phrasing and intonation.

Fluency bridges comprehension and word recognition. This is because fluency requires both recognizing most of the words on the page at sight (the word recognition part) and proper phrasing and intonation that reflects the author's meaning (the comprehension part).

Words per Minute

How fast should a reader be reading to be fluent? The usual standard is 90–120 words per minute. If a child is reading more slowly, there is probably a word recognition problem. That is, the student does not know all the words at sight. If a student is reading at more than 120 words per minute, it often sounds like speed reading—in which, by design, phrasing and intonation are not a concern. The exception to these generalities, of course, is the emergent reader of any age, who naturally reads more slowly at first.

It is difficult to read fluently in oral or silent reading situations if you must stop frequently to correct miscues. *Stopping* is a break in fluency, and you are no longer reading like you talk. Consequently, fast and accurate recognition of easily confused words is an important skill for fluency (see Example 22).

To read like you talk, you must also know what is going on in the selection being read. That is, you must comprehend the author's meaning in order to say the words the way the author intended them to be said (see Example 23 for guidance on explaining strategies for phrasing and intonation).

Phonics Is a "No-No" in Fluency

You do not teach phonics as a means to develop fluency. Phonics is analysis, and, as such, it is by definition a time-consuming task. If readers depend on phonics, they are slow and hesitant when reading. They cannot be fluent because they are stopping to sound out words.

Summarizing Fluency

Fluency is important because students seldom become enthusiastic readers until they experience what it means to be fluent. Reading just seems like too much hard work when you are not fluent.

The most important technique for developing fluency is ensuring that students do lots and lots of easy reading. Without lots of easy reading, students seldom develop the sense of what it feels like to be fluent. But in cases where lots of easy reading does not result in fluency, we should assess whether students recognize many words at sight and/or whether they use the words' meanings to determine voice inflection and phrasing.

What Do We Do for English Language Learners?

English language learners (ELLs) often are in particular need of explicit explanations. But what we teach such students is not different from what we teach an English-speaking child. Like English speakers, ELLs must learn word meanings, comprehension strategies, word recognition skills and strategies, and fluency strategies. The difference with ELLs is that we must put a very heavy emphasis on vocabulary (i.e., word meaning) and be more patient, more explicit, and more relentless in our explanations.

SUMMARY

When children have rich language backgrounds at home and come to school with lots of language background, there is less need for detailed explanations of skills and strategies. For struggling readers, however, explicit explanations are often necessary. The examples provided in Part II of this book can be used to guide your planning of vocabulary, comprehension, word recognition, and fluency lessons.

CHAPTER 3

Explaining the Forest as Well as the Trees

In Chapter 1, I used the old saying "The main thing is to keep the main thing the main thing" to emphasize the importance of engaging children in "real reading" tasks. In this chapter, I use the old saying "You can't see the forest for the trees" to convey another important aspect of successful reading instruction.

This book is dedicated to the idea that we should explain reading skills and strategies, especially when teaching struggling readers. But we must keep skills and strategies in perspective. If we get lost in the "trees" of skills and strategies and lose sight of the "forest" of larger understandings about reading, we often end up with students who can do skills and strategies but who do not become readers.

Another way to think about the "forest" is to think about skills and strategies as fitting inside a "bigger picture" about reading. The bigger picture includes understanding:

- Why we read and write.
- How the reading and writing system works.
- Why and when to use skills and strategies.

What We Mean by "Bigger Understandings"

If we teach someone to drive, we teach them the skills and strategies of driving, such as how to start the car, how to maneuver in traffic, how to parallel park, and so on. But we also teach "bigger understandings" essential to being a good driver. We teach that driving a car is a responsibility, not an inherent right; we teach conventions of driving courtesy; we teach the importance of using good judgment, and so on. Just as good driving teachers teach big understandings as well as basic skills and strategies, good reading teachers teach big understandings as well as basic skills and strategies.

So this chapter's message is that students must have important big understandings if they are to use skills and strategies well. Teaching crucially important big understandings is one of our most difficult jobs, but doing so determines whether students use skills and strategies well or whether they use them mechanically and without understanding.

Why Is It So Hard to Emphasize the Forest as Well as the Trees?

Remembering to emphasize the forest—that is, the "big picture" understandings within which skills and strategies are embedded—is one of a teacher's most difficult tasks, for two reasons. First, big picture ideas are often taken for granted, so they do not get discussed, listed, prescribed, or otherwise emphasized in the materials we use to teach reading. Second, accountability is often determined by testing students' knowledge of skills and strategies, but tests seldom measure larger understandings that determine the way in which skills and strategies are used. So we sometimes emphasize skills and strategies without ensuring that our students can fit them inside a big picture of reading and how it works.

Some students come to school already possessing many of the big understandings. But many do not. For those who do not, the big understandings must be demonstrated and talked about. The following sections describe how to demonstrate and talk about why we read and write, how the reading and writing system works, and why and when to use skills and strategies.

Talking about Big Understandings

Big picture understandings are concepts about reading and writing and how it works. These concepts can and should be developed by engaging students in activities and tasks that provide them with experiences in "living" what it means to be literate, such as projects, book clubs, readers' theater, and others. These are high-challenge tasks that give students experience with reading and writing as purposeful activity, so they are powerful ways to help students construct important concepts. But sometimes we must also supplement such tasks and activities with explicit talk. Struggling readers often have misconceptions about reading, and it is not always enough to engage them in activities. By also talking explicitly about big picture understandings, we help students understand the importance of such tasks and activities and how they contribute to becoming a successful reader and writer.

BIG UNDERSTANDINGS
ABOUT WHY WE READ AND WRITE

As described in Chapter 1, students develop understandings of the importance of reading and writing if they have opportunities to use reading and writing in important, sensible ways. Different teachers with different visions may have different views of what makes reading "important and sensible," and therefore may emphasize different reasons why we read.

But regardless of our particular visions, we should talk explicitly about the fact that we read to get an author's message. All reading and writing has message sending and message getting as its central purpose. We help students understand the message-sending and message-getting nature of reading by talking about the fact that anyone who writes is an author, that authors are writing messages, and that reading is a process of interpreting those messages.

The big understanding about the communicative nature of reading and writing can also be demonstrated by making explicit statements about activities such as the following:

- The exchanging of notes and the receiving of mail in the classroom mailboxes.
- Using response journals to communicate ideas and thoughts.
- Writing that is actually sent to someone.

Another reason why we read is because it is fun. We can build big understandings about this idea in the following ways:

- Read good literature to students on a daily basis, and in the process make explicit statements about the fun and joy of reading.
- Schedule daily DEAR (Drop Everything and Read) time or SSR (sustained silent reading) time and read yourself during this time, looking for opportunities to giggle or to smile while reading and then using these occasions to talk with the class about why reading is fun.
- Invite students to describe their own responses to reading, and help them make their own statements about the joyful features of reading.

Other techniques also build understandings about the importance of reading and writing. For instance:

- You may display posters of sports heroes and movie stars writing and reading and talk explicitly about why these famous people read.
- You and your students may compose stories to be placed in the classroom library, giving you the opportunity to talk explicitly about the fact that good writers are good readers and good readers are good writers.
- You may equip your classroom with beanbag chairs, cushions, sofas, and even a bathtub to engage your students in recreational reading and to give you an opportunity to talk explicitly about the joyful aspects of reading.
- You may bring in eggs to be hatched into chicks or cocoons that will become butterflies and then talk explicitly about how we can use books to find out more about what is happening.

Assessing Students' Big Understandings

How will we know that students possess big understandings? Like all assessment, the best assessment occurs when teachers watch their students during the normal course of the school day. For instance, when you observe things like the following, it is evidence that your students possess big understandings:

- ♦ They talk about reading and writing as a message-sending, message-getting activity.
- ♦ They talk about reading as useful in solving problems or accomplishing tasks.
- ♦ They talk about how various skills and strategies contributed to the successful completion of a task.
- ♦ They show evidence of being able to combine skills and strategies when reading.
- ♦ They talk about how they will use what they have read, or what they need to do next if a text did not provide the information needed for the task at hand.
- ♦ They show evidence of understanding that reading is a tentative, self-correcting process.

BIG UNDERSTANDINGS ABOUT HOW THE READING SYSTEM WORKS

Reading is not a random process. It is a system: a set of conventions we use to interpret and make sense of text. Basic skills and strategies are best applied within an understanding of that system. One way you can help build big understandings about the reading system is by talking to students about how reading works:

- • Talk explicitly about the top-to-bottom and left-to-right system of reading.
- • Describe reading as coded messages based on an alphabetic system.
- • While doing an experience chart about a recent field trip, point out how the white space between words tells us where one word ends and another begins.

- Make explicit statements about the importance of recognizing most words at sight while using phonics as an "emergency only" technique for figuring out a few unknown words.
- Describe reading and writing as reciprocal processes—writing is a process of sending a message and reading is a process of interpreting a message.
- Describe how the writer and the reader may operate from different sets of experiences and what good readers do to construct meanings despite these differences.
- Post a chart that illustrates the "before," "as you begin," "during," and "after" progression in comprehending, and refer to it often during instruction.
- Talk about "reading like we talk" and why it is important to change voice inflection when story situations change.
- Stop in the middle of a read-aloud to illustrate how, as good readers, we monitor our predictions and make new predictions as a selection unfolds.
- Make explicit statements about why we reflect after reading.
- Frequently talk about the fact that good readers use skills and strategies in combination and provide students with explicit examples.
- Describe explicitly the three different kinds of text authors use to convey their messages: stories (or narratives), information (or expository text), and directions (or procedural text).
- Be explicit about what features or attributes distinguish various genres of text (e.g., in the narrative category there are various forms of prose and various forms of poetry, while genres of expository text range from encyclopedias, to magazines, to newspapers).
- Be explicit about how writers organize text. Stories, for instance, are distinguished by a story structure that begins with a setting, a character, and a problem; proceeds through a series of events; and culminates in a resolution. Expository text can be structured as a chronology or as a comparison or as a number of other structures.

Examples of Teachers Explaining the Reading System

Kindergarten and first-grade teachers often read aloud large experience charts, running their finger under the print from left to right while saying, "Good readers start at the left and go across the print like this." Early primary-grade teachers sometimes allow note passing in their classrooms, and use this activity to emphasize in explicit ways the message-sending, message-getting nature of reading. Upper-grade teachers make explicit statements about the different text structures encountered in expository text. Teachers at all grade levels emphasize verbally (and then reemphasize, again and again) that good readers are assertive in building meaning and do not wait passively for meaning to come to them. All these big understandings help students see how the reading system works.

BIG UNDERSTANDINGS ABOUT WHY AND WHEN TO USE SKILLS AND STRATEGIES

It is important to know the names of skills and strategies and it is important to know how to do them. But of even greater importance is understanding when to use a skill or strategy, why you would use it, under what circumstances to use it, and for what purpose.

Comprehension provides a good example of this big understanding. Necessarily, we emphasize decoding in kindergarten and first grade. Lots of time is spent on learning to associate letters with sounds and to remember words at sight. But we do not want students to think decoding is the main thing. We want them to understand that if we say the words but do not get the meaning, we are not really reading. So it is crucial to keep making explicit statements about the importance of comprehension, even when teaching decoding skills.

Examples of Big Understandings about Why and When

We should be explicit about where and when to use structural analysis (only when there are root words, prefixes, suffixes, inflectional endings, and/or Greek or Latin roots) and where and why we use imagery (usually only in narrative text because that is where we usually find descriptive language). But a particularly prominent example involves the use of phonics. Primary-grade students often note the extensive amount of time they spend learning phonics and conclude, "If we are spending so much time on this every day, it must be that I'm supposed to sound out every word." But that, of course, is not what we want them to understand. Instead, we want them to understand that phonics is to be used only when one encounters an unknown word—that is, when a word is not a sight word.

A particularly subtle big understanding is that, in the end, knowing individual skills and strategies is not what counts. What counts ultimately is whether students combine all those individual skills and strategies into a cohesive package.

Students, however, often build a misconception based on their experience in school. Given the extensive amount of time they spend learning individual skills and strategies, they may quite sensibly conclude that the secret to good reading is "knowing" each separate skill and strategy. But, in fact, mature readers do not use skills and strategies separately. They combine individual skills and strategies into a more efficient package, and apply them quickly and effectively. They become strategic.

This is a real dilemma for teachers. Skills and strategies are basic tools. It is crucial that students, especially struggling readers, learn to use them. But even as we are teaching these individual skills and strategies, we must talk explicitly about the fact that while it is important to learn any particular individual skill or strategy, we will ultimately be combining skills and combining strategies to help us construct meaning more quickly and efficiently. The ultimate goal for students, therefore, is for them to apply skills and strategies as an efficient package. Communicating this idea is difficult. It requires lots of explicit teacher talk and lots of examples.

Examples of Combining Skills and Strategies

Using context and initial consonant sound to identify an unknown word in print is the most common example of combining skills and strategies (see Example 21 in Part II). But there are many other examples. The monitoring–questioning–repredicting cycle is a prevalent example in which strategies are combined and applied as if it was a single big strategy. When determining the main idea, readers combine predicting, monitoring, and repredicting; when using fix-it strategies, readers combine monitoring and a variety of other previously learned skills and strategies; when reading fluently, readers combine sight word recognition with "reading like you talk" (i.e., with comprehension). In sum, the key to expert reading is understanding how individual skills and strategies can be combined together to expedite efficient meaning getting.

SUMMARY

To us as teachers, many of the foregoing big understandings seem obvious. We sometimes think they are so obvious that no explicit talk is needed. That is, we take them for granted.

However, students who do not "catch on" easily often develop misconceptions about reading and writing. It is essential, therefore, to talk directly about these big understandings and to then ensure that students have many opportunities to apply them in the pursuit of authentic reading tasks.

CHAPTER 4

How to Use Part II of This Book

Part II is the heart of this book. It provides 23 examples of how to explain skills and strategies associated with vocabulary and comprehension, word recognition, and fluency. This chapter prepares you to use those examples.

Explaining Is Difficult

It is often difficult for us to provide explanations for how to read. To do so, we must be aware ourselves of the processes we use as we read. However, because we are expert readers, we no longer think about the processes we use to read. So because we are not ourselves conscious of those processes, it is not easy to explain the processes to our students. The examples in Part II of this book will, I hope, be a resource to you as you develop explanations of the mental processing involved in reading.

WHAT WE DO TO EXPLAIN

Explanations are our attempt to "demystify" the reading process for struggling readers so they can do what others appear to do effortlessly.

Explaining is not just "teacher talk" about how to do a skill or strategy. It is a four-step process.

1. The explanation must be based (as often as possible) in real reading tasks or activities.
2. Inside real reading tasks we provide information students can use to fill experiential gaps or to correct misconceptions or confusions about how to use skills and strategies to think one's way through text.
3. We scaffold student use of the information in subsequent responses to help them construct their own understandings based on the information we provided because students must ultimately "own" their skills and strategies if they are to be good readers.
4. We have students put the newly learned skill or strategy to work when doing the above real reading.

Explanations Are Assessment-Driven

We explain because we notice kids who are struggling with a skill or strategy. In that sense, explanations are assessment-driven. The best kind of assessment is a teacher watching and listening to kids as they read. We do not need a reading specialist to tell us, nor do we need to administer a formal test. The best judge of what a kid needs is an observant teacher. Each of the examples in Part II includes a suggested way to make such observations. The assumption is that explanations are provided in small groups of students who have been observed to need help with a skill or strategy.

HOW DOES EXPLANATION DIFFER FROM OTHER TECHNIQUES?

Most instructional techniques in reading are less intrusive than explicit explanation. The emphasis is on "guiding" or "coaching" or "discussing" in which the teacher assumes a less dominate role. These approaches often include no teacher explanation on the assumption that students will construct understandings about how reading works as they complete reading activities. That is, we expect students to "catch on" without explicitly saying, "This is how you do it."

It is true that some students do catch on without explicit help. It is not unusual, for instance, for average and above-average readers to figure out how reading works simply by engaging in reading activities. They "learn by doing." When learning by doing works, do it.

However, when students do not construct understandings easily, you should intervene with "how-to" information. This book is dedicated to that proposition.

TEACHING SUGGESTIONS INCLUDED IN EACH PART II EXAMPLE

To aid you in planning your own explanations, each example in Part II provides suggestions regarding each of the following eleven elements of explaining skills and strategies to students:

- Assessment before and after a lesson.
- Explaining the forest as well as the trees.
- Keeping the main thing the main thing.
- The student's objective.
- The "secret" to doing it.
- Lesson introduction.
- Modeling the thinking.
- Scaffolded assistance.
- Application in reading.
- Adapting the lesson to other situations.
- Application in writing.

Assessment before and after a Lesson

Explanations are always rooted in assessment. That is, we teach a specific skill or strategy because we have watched students read and have noted a particular need. Consequently, the assessment sections provided in Part II suggest what you might see to indicate that a skill or strategy needs to be explained and, following instruction, what you might look for to decide whether the explanation was successful.

Assessment is closely tied to application because the only assessment that really matters is whether students use what they have learned when doing real reading.

Explaining the Forest as Well as the Trees

Explanations sometimes fail because students lack certain "big understandings" of the kind described in Chapter 3. Consequently, each example in Part II includes a listing of big understandings we might need to explain.

Keeping the Main Thing the Main Thing

For illustrative purposes, each example in Part II is grounded in an imaginary reading situation. This situation describes an authentic purpose for reading a particular text. The point is that skills and strategies should not be taught in isolation. They should be taught in conjunction with real reading activity using real text, as noted in Chapter 1.

However, you cannot use the illustrative activity or the sample text as presented, nor are the examples appropriate for all classrooms or all grades. This book is a resource, not a script. Consequently, I expect the examples will be a source of ideas for you, but that you will use different text and different instructional situations in your own lessons, as I suggested in Chapter 1. For instance, skills and strategies might be grounded in projects designed to solve problems in the school environment, or skills and strategies might be grounded in pursuit of social changes. While there is no one way to do it, the guiding principle is that there should be a compelling purpose for reading.

Overcoming Students' Fear of Failure

When students struggle with one or another aspect of reading, it is difficult to combat their defensiveness and reluctance to try. Typically, struggling readers have experienced past failure. Like all humans, they try to avoid continued failure. Consequently, when explaining to struggling readers, you often hear kids say something like "I can't do this" or "I don't want to do this." Invariably their reactions are rooted in fear of embarrassment if they do not succeed. Overcoming student reluctance to respond requires teacher artfulness and sensitivity. As teachers, our instinctive response is to reassure students by telling them the task is easy. But, in actuality, we should say, "This is a hard task. Not everybody gets it right the first time." Doing so protects students' egos. If they fail to get it the first time, it is okay because it was hard, and not everybody gets it the first time. They are like lots of other people, and that's okay. When we tell them it is easy, however, students are not protected when they struggle. We told them it was easy, but for them it was hard. They feel dumb, and they will become even more reluctant to respond.

The Student's Objective

Explanation is intentional teaching. We intend to create a specific outcome in students. To do so, we need to be clear about what we are trying to accomplish. The best way to ensure that clarity is by making the objective public.

When students know what they are trying to learn, they are better able to learn it. Consequently, we tell students what they will learn and why. Each example in Part II includes an illustrative objective.

Objectives are stated so that we (and our students) can evaluate whether the objective was achieved. Our evaluation should be observable. That is, we (and our students) should be able to tell from watching or listening whether or not learning has occurred.

Using Observable Terms

A good objective focuses on what we want to see students do at the end of the lesson that they cannot do now. So we state the objective in terms of what we will see the student do. Since we cannot "see" invisible things such as "understanding," we do not use such terms. We use observable acts such as "stating" and "describing." Thus, an objective might be that students "will state a prediction and describe how the prediction was made." Because we can observe a student's statement and a student's description, we can determine whether instruction was effective.

The best way to begin an objective is like this:

"By the end of this lesson, you will be able to. . . ."

Then you go on to state exactly what students will be able to do, as in the example below:

"By the end of this lesson you will be able to make predictions before you read by using the title of the story as your clue, and you will be able to tell us how you made the prediction."

Because we want to avoid teaching skills and strategies in isolation from real reading, immediate application in real text should also be part of the objective statement.

"By the end of this lesson you will make predictions *about today's selection* before you read by using the title as your clue and tell us how you made the prediction."

By including application in the instructional objective, we avoid the trap of teaching a skill or strategy in isolation from its real use in text.

Making Objectives Public

Making objectives known to students helps them learn. In some schools, teachers begin every lesson by putting the objective on a 5" × 8"" note card or on piece of paper, posting it for students to read at the beginning of the lesson. Students and teacher then reexamine the objective at the end of the lesson to check to see if the objective was met. Making objectives public and explicit helps "demystify" the process of learning to read. Instead of students having to guess what they are accountable for in a particular lesson, they are provided with explicit information about what they are about to learn.

What Is the "Secret" to Doing It?

There is a "secret" (or "secrets") to doing any task successfully. For instance:

- A golf instructor teaches neophyte golfers the "secrets" to striking the ball correctly.
- A flight instructor teaches neophyte pilots the "secrets" to navigating an airplane under instrument conditions.

Reading, too, has its "secrets." But the secrets of reading well are more complex than the secrets for playing golf or flying an airplane because of the importance of background knowledge. The differences in background knowledge between teacher and student and the differences from student to student often means that different people will think differently about how to do a skill or strategy, particularly in comprehension. Consequently, when we give students a "secret" to doing a skill or strategy, it is presented as a representative example they can use to guide their efforts. It is not expected that every student will use what the teacher states in exactly the same way the teacher uses it. In short, being explicit does not mean being didactic.

Good readers often figure out the secrets for themselves. But this does not always happen with struggling readers. Reading tasks often remain a mystery for them. Directing them to the secret minimizes that problem. Given explicit information, they are better able to adjust what we say to their own way of thinking and to put it to work in the reading of real text.

The following are two examples of secrets:

- A secret to making predictions as one begins to read is to note the clues the author provides, think about what you know about those clues from previous experience, and then use that experience to guess what is going to happen. The reader says, in effect, "I've had experience with this topic, so, given what my experience is, what is likely to happen next here?"
- A secret to learning consonant letter sounds is to look at or point to the form of the letter while repeating the sound the consonant makes.

As teachers, we are expert readers; we read without conscious thought or effort. So we are sometimes at a loss to tell students what the secret is. The suggestions in the Part II examples are designed to help you as well as your students.

Introducing the Lesson

All students (but especially struggling students) learn best when they know what it is they are supposed to accomplish. So each example in Part II includes a sample introductory statement you can use to guide you in introducing your own explanations. Each includes statements of:

- A reference to the real reading being pursued (keeping the main thing the main thing).
- A statement of what students will be learning and how it will be used.
- A statement of the "secret" to doing it.

For example:

"We are reading this story today to collect information we can use in our project on whales. But we are also going to learn to use clues from the title to make predictions about what is going to happen in the story we read today. For each prediction, you will be able to tell me how you used the title as a clue to come up with your predictions. The secret to doing this is to examine the title, to think about what you already know from your experience with the topic, and to base your prediction on what your experience has taught you about it."

Students as Explainers

Explanation is sometimes erroneously associated solely with teachers. However, teachers are not the only ones with contributions to make. Often, students bring to the classroom valuable experiences and understandings about how to do things. Getting students to share their understandings about how to do reading tasks is an important explanatory resource.

Modeling the Thinking

Modeling how to read is not like demonstrating a physical task such as tying your shoes. We cannot physically demonstrate how reading works because reading is thinking. It occurs in the mind and is invisible.

The only way to model thinking is to talk about how to do it. That is, we provide a verbal description of the thinking one does or, more accurately, an *approximation* of the thinking involved (since there is no one way to do most skills or strategies). The information we provide gives students a "toehold" on how to do the thinking, and they gradually make it their own during the scaffolding that follows.

The Role of Modeling

Making sense out of reading is an individual process. No two people process information in precisely the same way. Therefore, modeling how to do a skill or strategy does not mean giving students rules to follow. Your explanation is, instead, *representative* of the thinking one does. Students use your explanation as a guide, not as a script to follow.

When we model, we provide a verbal statement of how to do a skill or strategy. We talk about the thinking we do in as clear and explicit a way as possible. Consequently, modeling is often described as "think-alouds" or as "mental modeling." We talk out loud about how *we* do the invisible thinking involved so our students can use our model as a starting point for developing their own way of doing it. To model, therefore, we should first have an awareness of what we do when we read and how we do it. Only then can we provide explicit models such as the following example of a think-aloud:

"Let me show you how to make predictions. Pay attention to what I do so you can use it as a starting point when you try to do predictions. When I make predictions, I look at the topic we are reading about and I think about what I already know about that topic and base my prediction on that experience. I say to myself, 'What does my experience tell me is likely to be happening in this story?' For instance, this story has the word *circus* in the title, so I think to myself, 'What do I already know about circuses?' Then I say, 'I have been to a circus. What happened when I went to the circus is probably what will happen in this story.' And so my prediction is based on what I already know from my experience."

Being Explicit When Modeling

It is difficult to be explicit when modeling. But the key to good modeling is providing enough information to "demystify" the process for students. For instance, when modeling how to make an inference, one teacher says, "I am thinking that they are afraid someone is going to see them." In the same situation, another teacher says, "Using my background knowledge, I know that I try to blend into my surroundings if I don't want to be noticed. So using what I know about that from my own experience, I infer that this person in the story is staying with the crowd so he won't be noticed."

The second example is a better model because the teacher makes her reasoning more visible by specifying how the text causes her to access personal knowledge and to then make an inference based on that background knowledge.

Each example in Part II of this book provides a sample of how we could use mental models or "think-alouds" about the skill or strategy in question. Each of those samples is tied to a particular piece of text, so you will need to adapt them to the text you are using. However, the intent of the example is to give you enough information for you to construct your own "think-aloud."

Scaffolded Assistance

Scaffolding is a process of helping students move from our modeling of the thinking to them doing the skill or strategy independently. Scaffolds are temporary supports. The idea of scaffolded assistance is to provide initial support and then to gradually reduce the support as the student gains confidence in responding. We give students opportunities to try out what we modeled, with lots of help from us at first, and then gradually with less and less help.

Because modeling usually provides students only with a toehold, they need scaffolds, or crutches, when they try to do what we modeled. The goal is to move from teacher ownership to student ownership. At first, students are dependent on our assistance. But as we gradually reduce the amount of our assistance, students gain experience in responding and build their own understandings. That is, they personalize the task and make it their own. They assume metacognitive control.

Metacognition and Explanation

Cognitive psychologists define *metacognition* as "thinking about one's thinking." It can also be described as "becoming conscious of your mental processes when using skills or strategies." Metacognition is an important part of explanation. The whole purpose in explaining is for students to become conscious of how to be successful when reading. In short, we want to put students in metacognitive control of their own thinking as they read. They are in control when they can describe how they used skills or strategies during real reading. However, a student must do more than mimic your talk. You must use judgment to determine whether what a student says is genuine understanding or just mimicry.

There are five keys to scaffolded assistance:

1. Using cues and crutches to focus students on key elements (that is, the "secret").
2. Gradually reducing the amount of assistance only when students show evidence of achieving the objective.
3. Observing each student's responses closely to determine how the student is making sense of the cues provided.
4. Changing or modifying a cue or crutch on-the-fly in response to students' restructured understandings.
5. Actually using the skill or strategy when pursuing real reading tasks.

Examples of Scaffolded Assistance

We used to teach swimming with "water wings"—balloon-like wings inflated with air and placed under the child's armpits. They kept the child afloat as he or she tried to swim. As he or she became more competent as a swimmer, the air in the wings was gradually reduced until the child was swimming without the assistance of the wings. The wings served as a temporary support, or scaffold. Similarly, young baseball players learn to hit the ball off a tee before facing a pitcher. The tee is a crutch, or temporary scaffold. In reading, scaffolded assistance may take the form of visual cues, or auditory emphasis, or leading questions by the teacher, depending on the nature of the task. These are crutches, or scaffolds, to help students get a handle on doing the task independently.

The length of time spent on scaffolded assistance depends entirely on how quickly students learn. Sometimes a student catches on after just a few responses, and sometimes assistance must be provided over several days or weeks. The key is to watch students' responses. If they respond satisfactorily, assistance can be reduced and ultimately eliminated. If they respond in ways that reveal confusion or hesitation, you may need to continue providing help and sometimes provide even greater support.

Each example in Part II of this book provides samples of how you might scaffold each skill or strategy. However, while the examples in Part II suggest scaffolding at three levels (one with extensive teacher help, one with less teacher help, and one in which students do the task with no help), your success in using these suggestions will depend on how skillfully you modify those suggestions to fit students' emerging understandings during the lesson. Teacher thought is essential because students respond differently to scaffolding. Consequently, you need to be ready to make spontaneous decisions about how to adjust the scaffolding if students demonstrate hesitancy, misconceptions, or misunderstanding.

The Need for Artfulness during Scaffolding

Students are always constructing understandings. They do so on the basis of their past experiences. Often these experiences are not congruent with what we say in our explanations. In those cases, students may restructure the information we provide and develop erroneous or misleading understandings. To minimize this, pay close attention to students' responses during scaffolded assistance, using student responses as "windows into their minds" to determine what sense they are making of the lesson. Often student responses during scaffolded assistance reveal a misconception or confusion. When that happens, adjust on-the-fly by altering the scaffolded assistance in ways that get students to construct a more accurate understanding.

Application in Reading

This section focuses on putting newly learned skills and strategies to use in real reading—that is, keeping the main thing the main thing. Application is an integral part of explanation because we cannot say an explanation has been successful until we see students transfer it to real reading. Hence, all the Part II examples have application built into the lesson objective and lesson introduction. Students know that application is the goal from the beginning of the lesson.

Application is the ultimate reason for providing an explanation. If students do not apply what they learned, the lesson is a failure. Learning skills and strategies without having a use for them makes no sense. By the same token, if a student is able to demonstrate a skill or strategy with scaffolded assistance but is not able to apply it independently when reading a real text, the lesson has not been successful.

Three different models for accomplishing application are illustrated in the examples in Part II. Some examples model how you can explain a skill or strategy and then have students apply it later when reading text; some demonstrate how you can teach a skill or strategy at the same time a text is being read; and some demonstrate how you can teach a skill or strategy after reading a selection. These models are provided for illustrative purposes. You will decide for yourself the kind of application to use in any particular lesson.

Adapting an Explanation to Other Situations

Each example in Part II assumes a particular grade level. Sometimes an example assumes an early primary-grade setting (K–2), sometimes it assumes a middle-grade setting (3–5), and sometimes it assumes an upper-grade or middle school setting (6–9). Additionally, some examples assume average students, others assume struggling readers in regular classrooms, and a few assume special education students.

From this initial resource, you will need to create your own lessons, adapting the suggestions to the level of your students. To assist you in making such adaptations, each example includes a brief description of how to adapt it to another grade level. For instance, if the lesson assumes a primary-grade situation, the example will include brief suggestions about how the explanation could be adapted to grades 3–5 or to a middle school situation; if the lesson assumes an upper-grade or middle school situation, the example will include suggestions for adapting the explanation to a primary-grade or middle-grade situation.

How Will You Know the Lesson Has Been Successful?

Each example ends with suggestions about how you will know if a lesson has been successful—that is, whether students are applying what they learned in the reading of real text. It is similar to the initial assessment that occurs prior to providing an explanation, but the focus is on not only being able to do the skill or strategy in isolation but, more importantly, being able to apply the skill or strategy in real text.

What If the Explanation Is Not Successful?

A reality of teaching is that not all explanations are successful. Especially when working with older struggling readers, it is often necessary to provide several explanations of the same skill or strategy for several days (and sometimes longer). When reteaching, it usually does not work to do exactly the same thing you did the first time. Use your professional judgment to decide where a lesson needs to be strengthened for particular students in particular situations. Does your description of the "secret" provide enough direction? Does your "thinking out loud" during modeling give the student enough guidance? Has the scaffolding been structured enough, and have the scaffolds been removed gradually enough? Does the student need more direction on how to use the skill or strategy in real text? Remember that good teaching means being relentless—when a lesson doesn't work one way, do it another way. But do not give up on the kid.

Application in Writing

Application is not limited to reading. Because reading and writing are reciprocal activities, most reading skills and strategies can also be applied in writing. Consequently, each example in Part II includes suggestions for how we might show students how to apply the skill or strategy when writing.

SUMMARY

As specified throughout this book, many students construct understandings about reading and how it works simply by engaging in literate activity. For some students, however, literate activity is not enough. They also need explanatory information about how to do various skills and strategies. It is for these students that the Part II examples are designed. I hope that they will be an adaptable resource you can use to develop your own explanations when students need more explicit help.

Is Explanation Just for Struggling Readers?

Explicit explanation is mostly used with struggling readers. But occasionally average and good readers also need explanations. Your decision to provide an explanation is a judgment call. Watch your students. If a student is learning without explicit explanations, do not provide explicit explanations. But if you see a student having difficulty, an explanation to "demystify" the situation may be helpful.

However, as I have frequently noted, the Part II examples cannot be used as a script or as a program. They are merely examples to get you started. As noted in the following chapter, your decisions when using Part II examples will determine their effectiveness.

CHAPTER 5

Decisions, Decisions, Decisions!

This book emphasizes the view that direct and explicit teacher explanation of reading concepts, skills, and strategies is an important alternative tool when students do not learn easily. I hope that you will find the 23 examples provided in Part II to be useful resources when explanation becomes necessary. However, before moving to Part II, I want to reiterate six additional and equally important messages.

First, and most important, our focus must be on students. While explanations temporarily put teachers in the "driver's seat," the instructional goal is to put students in control of their own efforts to make sense out of text. This means that we must, as soon as possible, get out of the way and ensure that students use explanatory information independently as they pursue authentic literacy tasks.

Second, effective reading instruction is an artful weaving of a complex tapestry. Good teaching consists of many elements, with the dominant one being an environment that engages kids in the highest forms of literacy activity. Instances of explicit instruction such as those I suggest in Part II are woven into the tapestry as relatively minor, though important, threads. So, while scientific research has "proven" explanation to be effective, good teachers situate it within an aura of warmth and authenticity rather than using it as isolated technical science.

Third, passion and artfulness are crucial aspects of effective teaching. Your students respond to your reading instruction to the extent that you care about their literacy development. They build a solid, enduring commitment to literacy to the extent that you creatively produce classroom opportunities to experience real reading and writing.

Fourth, explanation is not a panacea to be implemented mindlessly. As is the case with all instructional methods and techniques, success is determined not by the method but by how we use it. Explanation is no exception. It is merely a tool, one of many. It is effective to the extent that you use it selectively, thoughtfully, and adaptively.

Fifth, good reading instruction is balanced reading instruction. That is, explanation is not used exclusively; it is used selectively on an "as-needed" basis in combination with many other forms of reading and writing instruction. The exact nature of the balance—that is, exactly how much time you spend on various forms of instruction—is your decision. You are the one who knows best what your students need and what the local situation demands. So you are the one who must decide what "balance" is going to look like in your classroom.

Finally, effective use of explanations is a never-ending series of decisions. The Part II examples are not scripts or procedures. They require your proactive, assertive decision making. The following examples are illustrative.

DECISIONS ABOUT WHO GETS EXPLANATIONS WHEN

Explanation is a selective technique. You explain only for students who need it. It would be wrong to force a student who already possesses a skill or strategy to endure an explanation.

Consequently, using explanations presumes a diagnostic approach to teaching. Like a doctor who determines whether you are sick before prescribing medication, you determine whether students need explanations before providing them.

The Part II suggestions for before and after assessment will assist you in doing such diagnosis, as will the suggestions regarding "big understandings" that must be in place before explaining. If the data you collect indicate students already possess a particular skill or strategy, do not explain it; if the data suggest that students might profit from an explanation but that they lack necessary big understandings, develop those understandings before providing the explanation (or, alternatively, as you provide the explanation). This kind of diagnostic decision making must be an integral and uncompromised part of your use of explanation.

DECISIONS ABOUT HOW TO KEEP THE MAIN THING THE MAIN THING

It is difficult for struggling readers to grasp skills and strategies in isolation from their use in real-life tasks. Consequently, we constantly search for activities that engage students in genuine literacy tasks.

Finding such tasks is difficult because time is limited in classsrooms. Within the artificial environment of the classroom, teachers are expected to generate genuine real-life literacy experiences. This is no small task. Successful learning depends on it, however.

Some teachers accomplish this difficult task by establishing long-running projects or by forming semipermanent groupings such as book clubs or literature circles or classroom newspapers. Such activities motivate kids while also serving as readily accessible occasions for teaching skill and strategy instruction inside real reading tasks.

Motivating Kids to Read

It is difficult to motivate kids to want to read, especially kids who struggle. A literate environment, your passion for reading, and giving students a choice of what to read are all motivating. However, a powerful motivational tool in a teacher's arsenal is that of putting students in easy reading material. The major reason why many struggling readers hate to read is that they feel and look like failures when they read. Like all humans, students avoid situations where they look bad. So, if we want motivated readers, don't insist that they read difficult material unless you are right there to provide instructional support. Instead, put them in easy material and, when they read it, praise them lavishly. Even when students perceive such material to be "baby stuff," the feeling of success often overcomes their reluctance.

DECISIONS ABOUT WHAT TEXT TO USE

One of the essential messages of this book is that skill and strategy instruction should be accomplished in conjunction with real text. This is a particularly vexing problem because it is hard to locate appropriate text. No one text offers opportunities to put all skills or strategies to use, so you cannot just pick one at random. You must search for a text that affords opportunities to use the skill or strategy being learned.

Searching for such text is a time-consuming task. Teachers I work with often wistfully dream about how nice it would be if someone would just provide us with a list of the right texts. But, of course, doing so would eliminate the vitality associated with engaging students in reading tasks that they see as purposeful.

So, while text selection is often time-consuming and sometimes requires that we settle for less-than-ideal examples, it is nevertheless an essential part of effective explanations. Consequently it is another place where your own decisions are crucial.

DECISIONS ABOUT THE STUDENT'S OBJECTIVE

The objectives provided in each example in Part II are appropriate only for the imaginary situation in that particular example. Your own objectives will be grounded in the texts you select and in the particular variation on the skill or strategy students are learning.

DECISIONS ABOUT THE "SECRET" TO DOING IT

The examples in Part II are my best efforts to provide generic statements of what a "secret" might be for successfully doing various skills and strategies. I am confident that they will be helpful much of the time. However, because different students come from different backgrounds, and/or have different styles, and/or have idiosyncratic misconceptions, and because there is no universally perfect secret for any skill or strategy, my statement of "the secret" may not suffice in all cases.

Consequently, you must be prepared for students who, when you describe the secret, look at you in total puzzlement. It will happen, and when it does, you will need to modify the secret in response to students. What I provide is just a starting point. You should decide how to adjust it to fit the situation you face at the moment.

DECISIONS ABOUT MODELING THE THINKING

The examples of modeling I provide in Part II are tied to both the imaginary situation I create to keep the main thing the main thing and to an imaginary group of students. You will have a different situation, and you will have students you know. Consequently, you will need to decide how to fit the modeling to your situation and to your students.

Also, you will often need to adjust your modeling, shortening it or, alternatively, adding more detail, depending on the response of your students. For instance, some students may need an explanation but will not need as extensive a model as I suggest. Other students may need more detailed models, or may need repeated modeling. Such situations require that you make creative decisions about how to modify the suggested modeling.

Modeling versus Questioning

It is hard for us to resist questioning students while teaching. Our instinct is to use questions as a device to keep their attention. But if you have correctly assessed the situation, you know the students are unable to do the required task. So starting a lesson by asking them to do it is counterproductive. Instead, questioning should occur during scaffolding, following a brief period of uninterrupted teacher talk—your modeling. While this amount of teacher talk will be new to many students, they will respond well to it if you explain to them why you are doing such talking and that they will be much more fully involved in the scaffolding. It sometimes takes some time, but students soon adjust.

DECISIONS ABOUT SCAFFOLDED ASSISTANCE

As I emphasized in Chapter 4, scaffolded assistance requires much teacher thought and artfulness. In my own teaching, I find that no matter how carefully I plan the scaffolding, students' responses during instruction cause me to make on-the-fly adjustments. Sometimes students catch on quickly, and I can abandon some of the planned scaffolding; more often, they restructure my explanation in ways I had not anticipated, requiring me to create more extensive scaffolds and/or crutches.

Consequently, the three levels of scaffolded assistance I suggest are illustrative only. They will give you a start, but you will need to make proactive decisions of your own to ensure that your students receive the help they need to "own" the skill or strategy and to use it independently in real reading.

DECISIONS ABOUT APPLICATION IN READING

As I have emphasized throughout, explanations isolated from application in real reading are seldom helpful to students. You will need to decide how to adapt the suggested applications to reading and writing in your particular situation.

One of the most difficult aspects of application is finding the time for it. In my imaginary examples in Part II, lessons are not constrained by time limitations. But time is always an issue in real classrooms. So you will often need to parcel out lessons over several days, especially when working with struggling readers.

Your decisions about when and how your kids will apply what they learn in real reading and writing tasks will be crucial to instructional success.

Individual versus Combined Strategy Use

One of the trickiest decisions in teaching reading skills and strategies is how to help children combine them into fluid packages in which skills and strategies are used simultaneously as they construct meaning from text. Students who are highly verbal often learn to do this without direct teacher assistance. Others, however, must first learn skills and strategies as individual entities, and then have a teacher encourage them to combine them. An important decision point is when to help a struggling reader move from individual skill and strategy use to combinations. When that time comes, students will be greatly aided by your modeling of combined skill and strategy use and by your provision of scaffolded assistance during their first attempts to use combinations of skills and strategies.

DECISIONS ABOUT ADAPTING THE LESSON TO OTHER SITUATIONS

At all grade levels, reading skills and strategies can be learned in some authentic way by all students, including special education students. Because each example in Part II specifies a particular grade level or type of student or classroom organization, you must adapt my imaginary example to your grade level, to the type of kids you have, and to the way you have organized your classroom. The examples are useful as guides but cannot be used precisely as written.

DECISIONS ABOUT APPLICATION IN WRITING

Each example in Part II includes a suggestion about how the skill or strategy being taught could also be applied in writing. This is a frequently overlooked but powerful device for strengthening reading skills and strategies. From the very beginning stages of learning to read, we should make explicit to students how what we are learning in reading can be applied in writing. Doing so not only reinforces the big understanding about the reciprocal nature of reading and writing, but also helps students solidify their learning of skills and strategies. How you accomplish this integration of reading and writing, of course, will call for creative decision making on your part.

SUMMARY

In sum, an essential message of this book is that successful reading instruction requires proactive teacher decisions. Instruction, whether using explanations or other approaches and techniques, cannot be accomplished by passively following prescriptions or directions. You must "own" the instructional resource and mold it to your particular situation.

This is not bad news. It is good news. Teaching would be boring if all we had to do was follow directions mindlessly. It would be technical work, not professional work. Teaching is a profession because teaching effectiveness requires adjusting, adapting, creating, and making decisions in response to different situations.

So take this book and the resources provided in Part II and use them to create a literacy tapestry in your classroom that results in students who are not only skillful and strategic, but who also *do* read, and do so for authentic reasons.

Examples of How to Explain

Examples for
Explaining Vocabulary

EXAMPLE 1

Teaching Word Meanings Directly

There are two different kinds of vocabulary words. *Content words* describe concepts we can picture in our minds. For instance, because we have experience with bicycles and tricycles, we can picture them in our minds, describe them, draw pictures of them, and use the words correctly in oral and written language. *Function words* are words used to signal grammatical functions. For instance, words such as *the*, *into*, *from*, *is*, and *although* signal grammatical functions. We use these words in our oral and written language, but we do not "picture" them in the way we picture content words. They are normally learned through oral language experiences. Content words, on the other hand, must often be learned through direct explanation. This example describes one way to accomplish this.

Three conditions are important when you intentionally build content word vocabulary. First, vocabulary words are labels, and students must have experience with the concept the label describes. Direct experience with a word (i.e., experiencing it in reality, being able to touch it or feel it or experience it in some other real way) is best. Vicarious experience (i.e., reading about a concept or being told about it or seeing it in a video) is often the only way to experience a concept, but it is generally less effective than a direct experience. Having a cat as a pet is a direct experience; reading about a cat is a vicarious experience.

Second, learning meanings of new content words requires a focus on the features that distinguish the concept. For instance, a feature that distinguishes dogs is that they bark; a feature that distinguishes cats is that they meow. We have meaning for words when we link the word label with the features that distinguish that word.

Finally, we learn new word meanings when we have opportunities to use distinguishing characteristics to identify examples and nonexamples of the concept. For instance, the meaning of the word *dog* is strengthened when we use distinguishing features to determine whether something is an example of a dog or not.

The following is an example of how these three conditions can be used to explain word meanings to students.

How Will You Know You Need to Teach Word Meaning?

The situation: You are studying a particular content, and students are hesitant and unsure when using the words during discussions of the content.

The data you collect: Select words that are central to the content being discussed. Ask students to use the words correctly in sentences or to point to a picture illustrating the word. Word meaning needs to be developed if students cannot do so.

Explaining the Forest as Well as the Trees

Big understandings you might need to explain when teaching word meaning:

- That the things around us in the world have names, or labels.
- That these names or labels can be written as words.
- That every concept has particular attributes that distinguish its label from other words.

KEEPING THE MAIN THING THE MAIN THING

This example assumes a kindergarten class engaged in a math lesson. The teacher is going to share with the children a big book that has examples of basic geometric forms, such as squares, circles, rectangles, and so on (e.g., *Shapes and Signs*, by Tina Thoburn and Seymour Reit, Western Publishing, 1963). In preparation for sharing the big book, the teacher's goal is to intentionally and directly teach the meaning of each of the geometric words that will be encountered in the big book.

The Student's Objective

By the end of this lesson, you will be able to name and describe each of the shapes we find in the big book we are going to be reading together today.

What Is the "Secret" to Doing It?

Students must:

- ◆ Focus on features that distinguish one geometric form from another.
- ◆ Use the features to describe why a particular form is an example or a nonexample.

LESSON INTRODUCTION

Say something like:

> "Today we are going to read together a big book that has lots of different shapes in it. We are going to have to know what those shapes are in order to read the book together. So let me show you the names of each of the shapes and how I tell one from another.

The secret to naming these shapes is to pay attention to what makes one shape different from the other shapes. By the time we get done with the lesson, you will be able to name each shape and tell me how you know its name."

MODELING THE THINKING

Say something like:

"I have a bunch of wooden shapes here in front of me. Let's start with these two (*pick up a square and a circle*). Here's how I remember the names for these shapes. This one is a square. I know it's a square because it has four corners, and all the sides are equal. This one is a circle. I know it's a circle because it has no corners; it's all round. Pick up this one. Feel the four corners. Look at the sides. They are all equal. So, it is a square. Now pick up this one. Feel around it. It has no corners. It's all round. So, it's a circle."

SCAFFOLDED ASSISTANCE

Example 1: Extensive Teacher Help

Say something like:

"Let's look together at this wooden shape and decide what we see that will help us tell it apart from other shapes. This is called a triangle. Let's feel the corners together. Does it have four corners like a square? No, it has three corners. So, if a shape has three corners, we call that a triangle."

Example 2: Less Teacher Help

Say something like:

"Here's another shape. It is called a rectangle. Now we have to examine this rectangle to decide how it is different from a square, a circle, and a triangle. How many corners does it have? Yes, it has four, just like the square. Now look at the sides. Are all the sides the same? No, so let's decide how we can tell a square from a rectangle. What makes a square a square, and how do we know a rectangle is not a square?"

Example 3: No Teacher Help

At the third level of assistance, the teacher may simply name the wooden shape and invite the students to describe the features that make it different from the other shapes. For instance, the teacher may say something like:

"This wooden shape is called an oval. Let's look at it to see how it is different from the other shapes. What do you see that makes it different from a square or a rectangle or a triangle? What do you see that makes it different from a circle?"

APPLICATION IN READING

This is an example in which the teacher explains what is to be learned first and then has students use what they learned as they share together the big book the teacher will be reading to them. The teacher will then present on other days other books and activities that require naming basic geometric forms and describing how the students know one form from another.

Adapting This Example to Other Situations

Vocabulary development is an important part of reading instruction at all grade levels. Consequently, this kindergarten example can be adapted to other grade levels. For instance, a fifth-grade teacher who is teaching a unit on plant and animal life cycles using a science textbook (e.g., *Exploring Science*, Laidlaw, 1976) can use a similar approach in teaching vocabulary associated with life cycles.

HOW WILL YOU KNOW THE LESSON
HAS BEEN SUCCESSFUL?

You will know the lesson has been successful if students use the new words fluently in their oral conversations as they discuss the big book and if they can quickly and accurately point to visual and/or physical examples of the new words.

APPLICATION IN WRITING

The students in this example are kindergartners, and most of them will not be doing formal writing. However, they can make drawings and label those drawings using scribble writing or, if they are more advanced, printing. Since new words are solidified in the mind if they are used in writing, using the new words in this kind of writing should be encouraged. As a general principle, vocabulary is learned best if new words are used in writing as well as in reading.

EXAMPLE 2

Using Semantic Maps to Develop Word Meaning

As students progress in school, subject matter becomes more complex. Correspondingly, word meaning becomes more complex.

It becomes more and more difficult to provide direct experiences with new words because, instead of learning words by directly experiencing them, it is much more typical for new concepts to be learned through vicarious experiences. That is, we read about the new words and talk about the new words, but we do not directly experience them.

Second, vocabulary learning becomes more complex as kids progress through the grades because words are organized into categories and subcategories. While organizing ideas and concepts according to categories is "natural" in the sense that good verbal learners all do it, learning to categorize can be complex and difficult for some students.

Semantic mapping is one way to explain how to categorize word meanings. As in Example 1, it remains essential to identify key attributes distinguishing one word from another. But semantic maps provide the additional benefit of helping students visualize how word meanings can be categorized. The following is an example of how this might be done.

How Will You Know You Need to Teach Word Meaning?

The situation: You are studying a particular subject matter. Students often mix up words that belong in different categories.

The data you collect: Select content words that are central to a topic being studied. Ask students to group together those words that belong together and to describe why the words go together. If the students cannot organize words into sensible categories, an explanation of categorizing may be useful.

Explaining the Forest as Well as the Trees

Big understandings you might have to explain when teaching categorizing:

- ♦ That content words have key attributes that distinguish one word from another word.
- ♦ What is meant by classifying or categorizing.
- ♦ Why semantic maps can help us distinguish one word from another.

KEEPING THE MAIN THING THE MAIN THING

This example assumes a third-/fourth-grade combination. Students are working together on a science unit on rocks. Their ultimate goal is to take a trip to a local museum and to be able to identify the different rocks on display there. As part of their study of rocks, the teacher orally reads Joanna Cole's *The Magic School Bus: Inside the Earth* (Scholastic, 1987). In the discussion following the teacher's reading of the book, it is clear that students cannot distinguish among the various categories of rocks. The teacher decides to provide an explanation of how words can be organized into categories as a means for enriching word meanings.

The Student's Objective

By the end of this lesson, you will be able to correctly categorize different kinds of rocks we read about today and describe why certain rocks fall into certain categories.

What Is the "Secret" to Doing It?

Students must:

- ♦ Note how the words are alike.
- ♦ Note how they are different.
- ♦ Create a name for each category.

LESSON INTRODUCTION

Say something like:

"In *The Magic School Bus* story we just heard, Ms. Frizzle and her students found lots and lots of rocks. It is hard to remember the names of all those rocks. Let me show you how I remember these new words. The secret is to think about how they are alike, to think about how they are different, and to think of a single box with a single name that we could put certain words in and another box that we could put other words in. Let me show you how I do it with the first three words and then you can try it with other words."

MODELING THE THINKING

Say something like:

"When I am trying to understand the meaning of words like *sandstone*, *shale*, and *limestone*, I try to build a picture in my mind

of how the words are alike and how they are different, and then
I try to decide if something is an example of one of the words. I
can map the picture in my mind like this. I think to myself that
sandstone, shale, and limestone are all rocks. So they are alike in
that way, and I can show it this way:

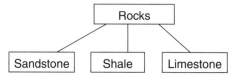

"But Ms. Frizzle said in the book that they are also alike because
they are all 'sedimentary' rocks. So, I can show that like this:

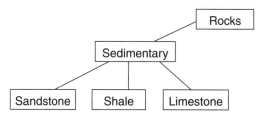

"So, I can say that these three rocks are alike because they are all
sedimentary rocks. My map of the words helps me with that. Now
I have to think about how these three rocks are different. One
way they are different is that they are different colors. Sandstone
is tan, shale is gray, and limestone is white. So, I can add to my
map like this:

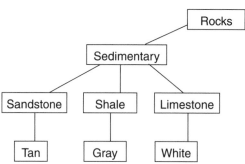

"But I learned from the book that these three rocks are also different because of what they are made of. Sandstone is made of

sand pressed together, shale is made of mud pressed together, and limestone is made of shells pressed together. So now I can add those to my map.

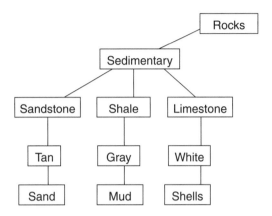

"So now I can tell which rock is which. They are all sedimentary, but sandstone must be tan and is made of sand all pressed together; shale would be rock that is gray and is made of mud all pressed together; and limestone would be rock that is white and is made of shells all pressed together.

"By looking for how the words are alike and how they are different, and then using that information to decide which is which, I am able to use the words correctly when I am talking and writing about rocks or trying to tell one rock from another."

SCAFFOLDED ASSISTANCE

Example 1: Extensive Teacher Help

Say something like:

"Remember when the bus sprouted a drill and went deeper into the earth? They found a different kind of rock down there. It was called 'metamorphic' rock. So I would have to put that on my map next to 'sedimentary.'

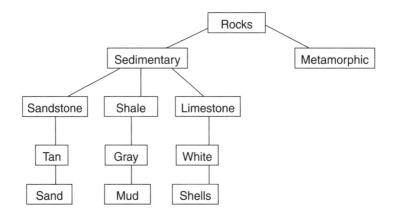

"So, then you need to think to yourselves, what rocks are 'metamorphic' rocks? Yes, marble and slate are both metamorphic, so I can put them on my map like this:

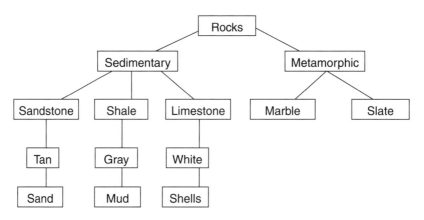

"So, how can you tell that a rock is marble or slate? I'll read this section to you again, and then we'll put what we find on our map. Yes, marble is harder limestone, and slate is harder shale. So let's put that on our map.

"So, how would you decide if a piece of rock was marble? Would it have to be hard? Would it have to look like the color of limestone? Yes. It cannot be marble unless it is very hard and unless it is a color like limestone."

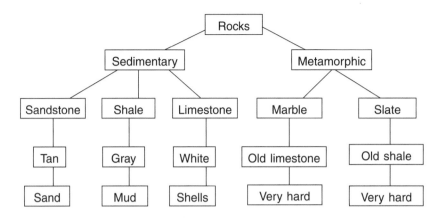

Example 2: Less Teacher Help

For a second level of assistance, you might continue to build the semantic map for rocks, using the igneous rocks described next in the book. This time, however, you would provide less direction. Say something like:

> "As Ms. Frizzle and the kids went deeper into the earth, they found another kind of rock. Let me read this section to you again, and then we will fill in the map together."

Example 3: No Teacher Help

At a third level of assistance, you may reread the section in the book on volcanic rock, remind the students to think about how these rocks are similar and what they would put on the map, how they differ from each other and how they would put that on the map, and how they would use what is on the map to determine what a particular rock is an example of. But you would leave it to them to do the actual categorizing.

APPLICATION IN READING

This lesson illustrates how explanations can be applied after a selection has been read. Because this is a unit on rocks, the teacher will present other books and articles to the students that contain the names of various kinds of rocks. In such future reading situations, the semantic map constructed in this lesson can be used to distinguish the various kinds of rocks.

Adapting This Example to Other Situations

This starter lesson assumes a group of middle-grade students. However, the same kind of semantic map can be used to build meaning for content words encountered in the upper grades and in middle school (e.g., in science or social studies). For instance, eighth-grade economics students using a text such as *Fearon's Economics* (Globe Fearon, 1995) to learn about the Federal Reserve System might construct a semantic map to delineate the distinguishing features of the system. The "secret" continues to focus on similarities and differences, with those used to identify examples and nonexamples.

HOW WILL YOU KNOW THE LESSON HAS BEEN SUCCESSFUL?

You will know the lesson has been successful if, in subsequent discussions during the unit on rocks, students use the new vocabulary words correctly in their oral discussion and in their writing.

APPLICATION IN WRITING

Vocabulary is strengthened by use. The more the new words are used, the more they are solidified in the mind. Vocabulary is particularly strengthened when new words are used in writing. Consequently, we should look for opportunities to have students use the new vocabulary words in their writing.

EXAMPLE 3

Using Context to Figure Out Word Meanings

One of the most efficient ways to increase vocabulary is to do lots and lots of reading. The more we read, the more word meanings we learn. The most efficient way to learn the meaning of a new word when reading is to figure it out through thoughtful use of context.

Context is a problem-solving strategy. When readers encounter an unknown word in text, they can use the clues embedded in the text around the new word to figure out for themselves what the word means. By learning this strategy, readers develop an enduring technique for increasing vocabulary independently and quickly.

Context clues range from fairly straightforward clues, such as direct definition clues, to subtle clues, such as mood clues. Children can learn to use the more obvious clues early, often during listening activities in the primary grades. More sophisticated context clues may not be learned until the middle and upper grades. Consequently, learning to use context clues is emphasized throughout the grades.

Context can be used as a decoding strategy—that is, for identifying words not recognized in print (see, e.g., Example 19). Its most enduring use, however, is as a tool for figuring out word meaning.

How Will You Know You Need to Teach Context Clues?

The situation: Students will be listening to text being read or will be reading text and will ask what a word means even though there are clues to its meaning embedded in the text.

The data you collect: Give students sample sentences that contain an unknown word and context clues to its meaning. Begin with sentences that are fairly obvious and move to more subtle clues. Students who cannot predict the meaning of the unknown words may profit from explanations about how to use context to figure out word meaning.

Explaining the Forest as Well as the Trees

Big understandings you might need to explain when teaching context clues:

- That when listening and reading, it is not unusual to encounter words we do not know.
- That when good readers get "stuck" on a problem during reading, they stop and figure out how to fix the problem.
- That some words have several meanings, and that we use context to decide which meaning is appropriate in that sentence.

KEEPING THE MAIN THING THE MAIN THING

This example assumes a group of four mainstreamed special education students in the second grade. They are involved in creating a school manual for what to do in severe weather, based in a science unit on weather. While the rest of the class is engaged in independent work on the weather unit, the teacher forms a temporary group of the four children. She wants them to read together the book titled *Tornadoes*, by Seymour Simon (HarperCollins, 1999). She has selected this book for two reasons: (1) the four children can use it to contribute important information about tornadoes in future class discussions on preparing the manual, and (2) the book provides several opportunities to apply the strategy of using context clues to figure out the meaning of words.

The Student's Objective

By the end of this lesson, you will be able to figure out the meaning of difficult words you encounter in the book *Tornadoes*, and you will be able to describe how you figured out the meaning of those words.

What Is the "Secret" to Doing It?

Students must:

♦ Identify the unknown word.

♦ Look back or look forward for clues.

♦ Use prior knowledge about the clues to predict the meaning of the new word.

LESSON INTRODUCTION

Say something like:

> "I have a book here on tornadoes. It will give us information we can use when we have a class discussion about what to put in our manual on severe weather. But before we start reading this book, I want to show you how to figure out some of the hard words you will find there. The best way to figure out the meaning of hard words while you're reading is to use the other words around the unknown word as clues. This is called 'using context.' The secret to using context is to use what you already know about other words in the sentence to predict what the unknown word means. Pay close attention to how I use context clues so you will be able to use the same strategy to figure out the hard words you will find in *Tornadoes*."

MODELING THE THINKING

Say something like:

"I'm going to use some sentences I made up to show you how I use context clues to figure out the meaning of new words. Pay attention to how I think my way through the problem because later I'm going to ask you to figure out some hard words using the same strategy. Let's use this sentence as an example:

The food was stored in a large larder.

"I am reading the sentence, but when I come to the word *larder* I stop because it is a word I have never heard before. I don't know what it means. So I say to myself, 'I wonder if there are some clues that would help me predict what *larder* means?' So I look back and read the sentence again. The sentence is about food, so that's a clue. And it says the food is stored, so that's a clue. I have prior knowledge about storing food. I know from my own experience that you store food in a cool, dry place, like a pantry or a refrigerator. So, *larder* must be a place like a pantry or a refrigerator. See how I used what I know about the clue words *food* and *stored* to predict what the new word means?

"Let me show you another example, and then you can try to do some. Let's say the sentence was:

The buoy floating in the harbor lit the water
and warned the ship to stay away from the rocks.

"I have never heard of *buoy* before. I don't know what it means. So I stop. I'm going to look for clues to its meaning. But this time I can't look back because there are no clues there. I must look ahead for clues. So I skip the word *buoy* and read on. I see the word *floating*—that's a clue. And *harbor* is a clue. And *lit* is a clue. And it says the buoy 'warned the ship,' so that's a clue. I know from my own experience what *harbor* is, and I know what *floating* is, so buoy is something that floats in a harbor. And then it says it is 'lit,' so a buoy must be a light. And then it says it 'warned the ship to stay away from the rocks,' and I know that ships don't want to hit rocks because they'll sink. So, using what I know about those clue words, I can predict that *buoy* is some kind of floating light that tells ships not to go near there."

SCAFFOLDED ASSISTANCE

Example 1: Extensive Teacher Help

Say something like:

"Now let's see if you can use context clues. I'll help you at first. Let's look at this sentence together:

> The wind shook the poplar so hard that some of its leaves fell to the ground.

"Okay, *poplar* is a new word for us. But let's see if we can use context to figure out its meaning. First, we have to read the words around the unknown word to see if there are clues that will help us. What is a word toward the end of the sentence that might help us? Yes, *leaves* might be a clue. Let's think about what we already know about leaves. Where do we find leaves? Yes, we know from our own experience that leaves are found on trees. So, if a 'poplar's' leaves were falling to the ground, what must a 'poplar' be? You used your experience with the clue word *leaves* to predict the meaning of a word you hadn't known before."

Example 2: Less Teacher Help

Say something like:

"Okay, let's look at another sentence, but this time I'm not going to provide so much help. The sentence is:

> The king laughed at the jokes and tricks performed by the jester.

"Read the sentence to see if there's a word you don't know. Okay, if you don't know the word *jester*, can we use context to solve the problem? What would we do first? Yes, we look back for clues. Are there words in that sentence that you could use as clues? Yes, *king* is a clue. Do you have knowledge about kings? So that will help us. And, yes, *jokes* is a clue. We know what jokes are. And *tricks* is a clue. We know what tricks are. So we must use our knowledge about 'kings' and 'jokes' and 'tricks' to figure out what a jester might be. What do we know about someone who performs jokes and tricks for someone like a king? Yes, we might call them 'clowns.' Does 'clown' make sense in that sentence as a meaning for *jester*?"

Example 3: No Teacher Help

Once students have appeared to grasp the idea, provide a sentence containing an unknown word and ask students to describe for you how they would figure out the new word. They should not only identify a meaning for the new word but also state how they figured it out.

APPLICATION IN READING

This example illustrates an application model in which the students learn the strategy first and then apply it to a real reading situation. The real reading situation in this case is reading *Tornadoes* in preparation for contributing to a class manual on severe weather. After learning about context clues, the four students read about tornadoes but also figure out new words for themselves as they read. For instance, the teacher may direct them to the word *funnel* on the first page and review with them how the clues "huge elephant's trunk" and "giant vacuum cleaner" can be used to predict the meaning of *funnel*.

Adapting This Example to Other Situations

This example assumes a small group of second-grade special education students who need to learn to use fairly obvious context clues to read an expository text on tornadoes. However, context clues can also be taught to students in higher grades who are reading narrative text that requires the use of more subtle context clues. For instance, when fifth graders are using a book such as Meindert

DeJong's *The House of Sixty Fathers* (HarperCollins, 1956), context clues can be taught to determine the meaning of words having multiple meanings—such as *steal* in a sentence such as "Tien Pao started to steal away" and such as *rooted* when "Glory-of-the-Republic rooted about." Similarly, and at a still more sophisticated level, when middle school students are using a book such as Lois Lowry's *The Giver* (Houghton Mifflin, 1993), context clues can be employed to determine the subtle differences between *distraught* and *distracted* when the instructor chastises Asher in Chapter 1 and, later on the same page, when Jonas tries to decide whether he is "frightened" or "apprehensive." While the thinking is more sophisticated in these two examples, the teacher's explanation emphasizes basically the same "secret"—namely, using what we already know about the clues surrounding the difficult word to figure out what the words mean in that context.

HOW WILL YOU KNOW THE LESSON HAS BEEN SUCCESSFUL?

In the example provided, you will know the lesson has been successful if the four students, after reading *Tornadoes*, use the new words encountered in the text during their discussion with the class. Also, you will know the lesson has been successful if the four students can describe the thinking they used to figure out the unknown words.

APPLICATION IN WRITING

Students can also use context clues in the writing they do themselves. For instance, in writing stories for reading aloud to classmates, students can be encouraged to include words that are likely to be new to their listeners, but to also include around the new words some clues the listeners can use to figure out the new word's meaning. This application is quite difficult, however, and is more applicable to older students. Even in those situations, students will need to use examples from real text as models when they try to incorporate context clues into their writing.

Structural Analysis

Structural analysis is figuring out what a word means by examining its meaning units, a process linguists call "morphemic analysis." There are four kinds of structural units, or morphemes, useful in figuring out the meaning of unknown words: (1) the compound word *snowman* is made up of two morphemes or meaning units—*snow* and *man*; (2) prefixes and suffixes are meaning units (e.g., the prefix *un* in *unhappy* means "not," and the suffix *-ful* in *joyful* means "full," as in "full of joy"); (3) inflectional endings such as the plural *-s* and the ending *-ed* are morphemes that signal meaning (the plural *-s* means more than one and the ending *-ed* means something happened in the past); and (4) older students often learn to use Greek and Latin roots to identify words containing those elements.

When an unknown word is made up of structural units, or morphemes, structural analysis can be a quick and efficient way of figuring out the word meaning. However, it is only useful when structural units are present. Consequently, an important element of teaching structural analysis is emphasizing that it works only when a word contains morphemes, or structural units.

This example focuses on compound words. It can be adapted to explain how to use prefixes, suffixes, inflectional endings, and Greek and Roman roots.

How Will You Know You Need to Teach Structural Analysis?

The situation: Students are reading and, upon encountering an unknown word containing a structural unit, are unable to figure out the meaning of the word.

The data you collect: Ask students to point to words in text that contain structural units and to say the meaning of the word.

Explaining the Forest as Well as the Trees

Big understandings you might have to explain when teaching structural analysis:

- That words can be made up of a combination of two or more meaning units.
- That there is a difference between a meaning unit and "a little word in a big word" (i.e., in the word *father, fat* and *her* are not meaning units and cannot be used to figure out the meaning of the word).
- That sometimes a letter combination may look like a meaning unit but is not (e.g., the *un* in *under* is not acting as the prefix *un* in that word and cannot be used to figure out the meaning of the word).
- That structural analysis can be used aa a strategy only if a word is made up of meaning units.

KEEPING THE MAIN THING THE MAIN THING

This lesson is being taught to a small group of learning-disabled students in second grade. The class as a whole is working on an ecology unit in which the end goal is to produce an exhibit for the school's science fair. Because these struggling readers do not yet have independent reading levels, the teacher is guiding their reading of *The Sea Otter*, by Maggie Blake (Wright Group, 1996), The primary reason for reading this expository text is to gain information for use in creating the science fair exhibit. However, because these students have not yet learned to figure out word meaning using structural analysis, and because the text contains many compound words such as *shellfish, fishermen, seaweed, waterproof, underwater,* and *playground,* the teacher decides to explain how to use compound words in conjunction with the reading of the text for ecological information.

The Student's Objective

By the end of this lesson, you will be able to use structural units to figure out the meaning of an unknown compound word in today's book on sea otters, and describe how you did it.

What Is the "Secret" to Doing It?

Students must:

◆ Decide whether the unknown word is made up of two known words.

◆ Put the two known words together to predict what the compound word means.

LESSON INTRODUCTION

Say something like:

"As part of our ecology project for the science fair, we are reading *The Sea Otter* to find out how otters relate to other creatures in the world. But when we read this book together, we are going to find some hard words that we don't know. So, before we start, I want to teach you how to figure out the meaning of words like these. These are special words that are made up of two other words you already know. When words are made up of two other words, we call them "compound words." The secret to figuring out what a compound word means is to find the two smaller words you know in it and then combine those words into a single meaning."

MODELING THE THINKING

Say something like:

> "Watch me while I show you how you how I figure out the meaning of compound words (*write this sentence on the board*: "I made a big snowman on the playground today.") When I am reading along and come to this big word that I've not learned yet [*snowman*], I try to figure it out myself. I think, 'When I look at this word, it has in it the word *snow*, which I know, and it has in it the word *man*, which I also know. I'm circling each of those words so you can see that the compound word *snowman* is made up of the two smaller words *snow* and *man*. So, if I put those two words together, they say "snowman," which means "a man made of snow." I figured out what this compound word means by looking to see if it had words in it I already know, and then I said the two words I know together."

SCAFFOLDED ASSISTANCE

Example 1: Extensive Teacher Help

Say something like:

> "Now let's see if you can do one if I give you some help. In the same sentence with *snowman*, there is another big word (*point to playground*). I'm going to help you this time by drawing circles around the two parts of the big word (*circle* play *and* ground). What does the word in the first circle say? Yes, that word is *play*. What does the word in the second circle say? . . . Yes, that word is *ground*. So we know the meaning of both small words. Put them together. What does the big word *playground* mean? Yes, it means ground that we play on. Is that a word you use? Where is our playground? Because it is made from two words we know, *playground* is a compound word. How did we figure it out? Yes, we found little words we know in the big word."

Example 2: Less Teacher Help

Say something like:

> "Now let's see if you can figure out the meaning of compound words when I give you less help. In the book we will read today we will find lots of new words. One of those words is *mussel* (*write it on the board*). Another is *underwater* (*write it on the board*). Let's see if we can use what we know about compound words to figure out these words. Look first at this word (*point to* mussel). That's a word we don't know, so we try to figure it out using what we know about compound words. We can't because that word is not made up of little words that we already know the meanings of. Now look at this word (*point to* underwater). We don't know that word either, so we try to figure it out. Can we use what we know about compound words? Yes, we know the word *under*, and we know the word *water*. So, if we say them together, what do we get? Yes, this is the word *underwater*. It means that something is under the water. Say again how you figured out the meaning of *underwater*. But, remember, not all words are compound words. *Mussel* wasn't a compound word. So we use this strategy only when we see that a word is made up of two words we already know."

Example 3: No Teacher Help

If students are responding well with teacher help, the guided reading of the book *The Sea Otter* can begin. As compound words are encountered in the text, students are asked to figure out their meanings, using what they have learned.

APPLICATION IN READING

This is an example in which a skill or strategy is taught before reading the text where it will be applied. Continued application will occur on subsequent days when the group of students encounters other text containing unknown compound words.

Adapting This Example to Other Situations

Compound words are normally learned during the earliest stages of reading. However, other forms of structural analysis, such as using prefixes, suffixes, inflectional endings, and common Greek or Latin roots, are often learned in second, third, or fourth grade. When it is necessary to explain how to use such structural units to figure out word meaning, a process similar to the example described here can be adapted and used.

HOW WILL YOU KNOW THE LESSON
HAS BEEN SUCCESSFUL?

You will know the lesson has been successful if, when students encounter an unknown compound word, they can say a correct meaning for the word and can describe how they figured it out.

APPLICATION IN WRITING

Understandings about compound words and other structural units can be applied to writing as well as to reading. When writing the report that will be part of the science fair exhibit on ecology, for instance, these students may need to spell words such as *underwater*, *shellfish*, and *seaweed*. When faced with this task, they can use knowledge of structural units, first spelling the known word that is the first part of the compound and then spelling the known word that is the second part of the compound.

Examples for Explaining Comprehension Strategies

Predicting

Predicting is fundamental to comprehension. Good readers anticipate meaning. They do this by predicting what they think is going to happen in the selection and by revising their predictions as they read.

Readers of all ages make predictions. Preschoolers and kindergartners make predictions as they are listening to stories being read to them. More proficient readers make predictions when they are reading expository text. Consequently, predicting can be taught to kindergartners and to high schoolers alike, and it is appropriate in various genres of narrative text as well as in various forms of expository text.

As with all comprehension strategies, predicting is based on the thoughtful use of prior knowledge. Readers make predictions based on purpose for reading, topic clues, and the type of text being read. This example focuses on using topic clues to make predictions. That is, readers use their prior knowledge about the topic as the basis for making the prediction.

How Will You Know You Need to Teach Predicting?

The situation: Students keep on reading even when what they are saying no longer makes sense. When you ask "What will happen next?" they make no response.

The data you collect: Interview students about what they are think-ing as they begin to read or what they think was going to happen next. If their responses indicate that they are not anticipating mean-ing, an explanation may be helpful.

Explaining the Forest as Well as the Trees

Big understandings you may need to explain when teaching pre-dicting:

- That meaning getting is the purpose of reading.
- That one must actively construct meaning—it will not hap-pen without effort.
- That predicting is an example of how readers actively con-struct meaning.
- That predicting is not a wild guess—it is a thoughtful hypothesis based on clues.
- That like all comprehension strategies, predicting is a mat-ter of "reading between the lines," or inferring, using prior knowledge.

KEEPING THE MAIN THING THE MAIN THING

This example assumes a group of fifth-grade students who are doing a project on point of view, especially as it relates to how history is viewed differently depending on your particular perspective. One of the events they have been reading about is Custer's Last Stand. Now they are going to read Paul Goble's *Red Hawk's Account of Custer's Last Stand* (University of Nebraska Press, 1992). Because these are students who in previous observations have not been anticipating meaning, the teacher plans to explain predicting using topic clues.

The Student's Objective

By the end of this lesson, you will be able to use topic clues the author provides and what you already know to make predictions when reading the book *Red Hawk's Account of Custer's Last Stand*, and you will be able to tell how you did it.

What Is the "Secret" to Doing It?

Students must:

♦ Look for clues to the topic.

♦ Think about what they already know about the topic.

♦ On the basis of their prior knowledge, predict what they think will happen.

LESSON INTRODUCTION

Say something like:

"We have been learning about different points of view regarding various famous historical events, such as Custer's Last Stand. Today, we are going to read more about Custer's Last Stand. But before we start, I want to show you a strategy that will help you understand more of what you read in this book. This strategy is called 'predicting,' which means to think ahead about what is going to happen in the selection. The author always provides clues to what the topic is. One secret to predicting is to find topic clues, to then think about what you already know about that topic, and to use what you know to predict what you think will happen. We're going to read this book together, and, as we get into the book, I am going to expect you to use your prior knowledge about the topic to make predictions as we go along."

MODELING THE THINKING

Say something like:

> "Before we start reading, let me show you how I make predictions. I already know we are going to be reading about Custer's Last Stand. The book we are going to be reading is titled *Red Hawk's Account of Custer's Last Stand.* As a good reader, I immediately start making predictions about what is going to happen here. I start by using the clues to the topic in the title. The author says this is 'Red Hawk's account.' I use that clue to think about what I already know about 'Red Hawk' and what predictions I would make based on what I know. I say to myself, 'I know from my previous experience that 'Red Hawk' sounds like a Native American name, so I predict that Red Hawk is an Indian. And because we are studying point-of-view, I predict that this is a Native American's story of Custer's Last Stand, not Custer's view.' See what I did to predict? I used the clue the author gave me and what I already know about that clue to make the prediction."

SCAFFOLDED ASSISTANCE

Example 1: Extensive Teacher Help

Say something like:

> "All right, now let's try one together. On page 4, a section begins with the title 'General Custer.' We know that to predict we need to begin with topic clues the author provides. Is the author providing a topic clue here? What is the topic going to be?
>
> "Once we identify a topic clue, we need to access our background knowledge about that topic. What do we already know about Custer? We know he was a cavalry officer who died in a battle with the Sioux and Cheyenne in 1876. Now, use what you already know—that this is a book about his last stand, as told by one of the Sioux he was fighting against. If you were Red Hawk, what would you be telling about here? You use your experience of what you know and what you would do to predict what is going to happen here."

Example 2: Less Teacher Help

Say something like:

> "On the next page there is a quote from Sitting Bull that says, 'I tell no lies about dead men. Those men who came with Long Hair were as good men as ever fought.' This is a topic clue the author is providing for you. Can you use this clue and your prior knowledge about the words Sitting Bull uses to predict what is going to happen next in the selection?"

Note: Again, when they predict, have the students explain how they used their prior knowledge in combination with the topic clue.

Example 3: No Teacher Help

As students progress, you may just want to mention the importance of the clue and of accessing background information and then have students identify a clue, make their predictions, and state their thinking as they predict without further assistance from you.

APPLICATION IN READING

This example illustrates how a strategy can be taught using the selection being read. So the strategy learning and the application in text occur simultaneously. In future reading, of course, you would continue to cue students to the topic clues provided by the author and the way readers use prior knowledge to make predictions about what is coming.

Adapting This Example to Other Situations

This example assumes a fifth-grade situation. However, predicting can be taught at any level. For instance, primary grade teachers can adapt this fifth-grade example to teach first graders to predict using topic clues when reading stories such as Maurice Sendak's *Where the Wild Things Are* (HarperCollins, 1976) to their students.

Similarly, this example can be adapted when teaching students to make predictions using text clues or purpose clues. The secret continues to be application of prior knowledge, but the focus is on prior knowledge about text or about the purposes of reading.

HOW WILL YOU KNOW THE LESSON HAS BEEN SUCCESSFUL?

In subsequent reading, students will report that they made predictions and will state those predictions. When you ask them how they made their predictions, they should report the topic clues they were using and how they used their prior knowledge about each topic clue to figure out what might happen next.

APPLICATION IN WRITING

Remind students that when they write, they are authors. Authors provide topic clues the reader can use to make predictions about what is coming next. So, when they are writing, students should be conscious of the clues they are providing the reader.

Monitoring, Questioning, and Repredicting

Comprehension is an active cycle of mental activity. It starts when readers *anticipate* meaning by predicting ahead of time what they will find in a passage. But predicting is only the beginning of the process of seeking meaning. As readers move into the text, they monitor, they question, and, when necessary, they abandon the prediction they made earlier and make a new prediction. In short, good readers do not sit back and passively wait for meaning to come to them. They talk to themselves about the meaning they are building. Because all three strategies—monitoring, questioning, and repredicting—happen together, they are taught together in this example.

Monitoring is a process of talking to oneself about whether the meaning being encountered is the meaning anticipated—that is, whether the original prediction is coming true. Monitoring and questioning are virtually the same, because *questioning* is also a process of talking to oneself about whether the meaning makes sense. That is, the reader is constantly asking, "Does this make sense? Is this what I had predicted was going to happen?" If the answer is "No," then the reader begins self-talk about what new prediction needs to be made, given the new information encountered in the text. The readers says something like, "Given what I'm reading here, and my prior knowledge about information like that, what must I *now* predict is going to happen?"

All this mental activity happens in a flash—almost instanta-
neously. Good readers seem to do it "naturally" with no apparent
effort. However, struggling readers often operate under the misconception that meaning will "come to them" as they decode words; they
do not understand that meaning getting requires active probing for
meaning. These students may need explicit information about how
this seemingly instantaneous mental activity works.

In sum, monitoring, questioning, and repredicting are the strategic heart of the comprehension process. But this cycle of thinking
is difficult to teach. First, the process not only happens in a flash, it
also is invisible. Second, it is personal—students cannot exactly mimic
what you do because the process depends on individual prior knowledge. Third, it is tentative—predictions are made and then must be
abandoned and replaced by new predictions. Finally, it takes energy—
readers cannot coast along passively.

How Will You Know You Need to Teach Monitoring, Questioning, and Repredicting?

The situation: Students' reading does not sound like talk because
they are just decoding words. When asked questions about the predictions they made, they guess or do not answer at all.

The data you collect: Ask students to describe for you what they
were saying to themselves as they read the text. If their responses
indicate that they are not monitoring their predictions or questioning whether the meaning makes sense in light of the prediction, or
are not changing their predictions as needed, an explanation of this
strategy may be needed.

Explaining the Forest as Well as the Trees

Big understandings you may need to explain when teaching
monitoring–questioning–repredicting:

- That comprehension is an active, probing process.
- That predicting is only a first step.

- That predictions change as we read.
- That predicting–monitoring–repredicting is a cycle that is repeated over and over again.

KEEPING THE MAIN THING THE MAIN THING

This example assumes a middle school literature class. The students are about to begin reading Sharon Creech's *Walk Two Moons* (Harper Trophy, 1994) as part of an ongoing discussion of what it means to be human. However, the teacher also wants to use the first chapter of *Walk Two Moons* to explain the monitoring–questioning–repredicting cycle that is essential to comprehension.

The Student's Objective

By the end of this lesson, you will be able to describe how you talked to yourself as you monitored, questioned, and repredicted during the reading of the early chapters of *Walk Two Moons*.

What Is the "Secret" to Doing It?

Students must:

- Keep the original prediction in mind.
- Keep asking whether that prediction continues to make sense in light of new information in the text.
- Use new information in the text and prior knowledge about that information to make new predictions.

LESSON INTRODUCTION

Say something like:

> "As we read *Walk Two Moons* to add to our growing understanding about the love and hurt and emotions associated with being human, we also want to do what good readers do—we want to be active and aggressive in building the meaning in the story. Once we make our first prediction about what is going to happen, we must continue to monitor what we read and to question whether what we are finding is what we expected to find. Often, your monitoring and questioning will mean that you must 'trash' your original prediction and create a new one that fits the new clues you are finding in the text. The secret to doing this active thinking as you read is to talk to yourself as you read, questioning whether the prediction you made continues to fit what you are finding in the text. When you find your prediction no longer fits, you must make a new prediction right there in the middle of the text. I'm going to show you how to do this as we read the first chapter of *Walk Two Moons* together. Then you will show me how you do it later in the chapter."

MODELING THE THINKING

Say something like:

> "By looking at the title and the clues following the title page, we have already decided that 'walk two moons' must be part of a Native American saying: 'Don't judge a man until you've walked two moons in his moccasins.' So we have predicted that this must be a story about not making judgments about other people. So let me show you how I talk to myself as I begin reading the chapter.
>
> "As I read page 1, I find out that this story is being told by a girl who moved from Kentucky to a new house in Ohio. Immediately, I am questioning, saying to myself, 'This doesn't seem to have anything to do with judging other people. Maybe that will come later. Right now, this seems to be about a girl who is mov-

ing.' So I've already changed my prediction. I predict this is a story about moving. So I read on.

"As I get to the bottom of page 1 and to the top of page 2, I am monitoring what the girl is saying. What the girl says about 'no trees' and 'houses all jammed together' are clues. In my prior knowledge, if I said things like that, it would mean that I was unhappy and perhaps complaining. So that makes me think that I should alter my prediction to something about the girl being unhappy about moving.

"But, even as I'm making this new prediction, I'm asking myself questions: 'Who is this red-haired lady named Margaret? Could it be the girl's mother? But the girl doesn't want to greet the red-haired lady.' That's a clue. If that were me, I wouldn't be acting that way if she were my mother. I would act that way if the person were someone I didn't know. So I would make still another prediction: 'No, it couldn't be the girl's mother because the girl doesn't want to go up on the porch and see her.'

"But then I think again about my original prediction about 'walking in someone else's moccasins.' I say to myself that maybe what is going to happen is that the girl is going to find out that she shouldn't judge the red-haired lady.

"Do you see how I am talking to myself as I read? I make a prediction, and then I ask questions about whether my prediction is still making sense. If as I read along I encounter new information that seems to say that my original prediction doesn't make sense, I modify my prediction or sometimes I make a whole new prediction, based on the clues and my prior experience with those clues. Now let's see if you can do as I did as we read on in Chapter 1."

SCAFFOLDED ASSISTANCE

Example 1: Extensive Teacher Help

Say something like:

"All right, as we read down to the bottom of page 2, we monitor what is happening, and we find that there is someone else we should be paying attention to. The girl telling the story says there is 'a round girl's face' in the upstairs window. You should be asking yourselves questions about that. Are you asking what that little girl has to do with the story? It says she 'looked afraid.' Are you asking why she looked afraid? It goes on to say that this new little girl will become her friend. So let's think about our prediction. Can you ask yourself whether this might have anything to do with walking in someone else's moccasins? Could it be the little girl that is the focus and not the red-haired lady? Let's make a new prediction, something about the fact that this is going to be primarily a story of the girl's friendship with Phoebe and not of the girl's relationship with the red-haired lady."

Example 2: Less Teacher Help

Say something like:

"All of a sudden, in the next paragraph we are hearing about 'being locked in a car with my grandparents.' That's a strange change in meaning from resisting meeting the red-haired lady or meeting Phoebe. Are you questioning, saying this isn't what you expected? But we have to try to make it fit. Are there clues we can use to make a prediction that fits? Yes, it sounds like the girl is going to tell her grandparents a story about Phoebe. So what does that make us predict about 'walking in someone else's moccasins?' Yes, maybe this *is* a story about Phoebe more than a story about the red-haired lady. Maybe. But the last sentence also should cause you to ask questions again. Yes, you should be questioning why a story about Phoebe would be like the plaster wall in the girl's old house in Kentucky."

Example 3: No Teacher Help

As students become comfortable with the thinking, direct them to read the remaining pages in the chapter and to report how they talked to themselves during that section. They should report instances where their monitoring caused them to pause and question, and they should report what they were thinking about. And they should report where they started making new predictions and how they combined the text clues with their prior knowledge to make those predictions on-the-fly as they were reading. By the end of the chapter, they should be questioning their earlier prediction that this is going to be a story about Phoebe.

APPLICATION IN READING

This example illustrates how a strategy can be taught as the teacher and the students read a text. As the class moves into subsequent chapters of *Walk Two Moons*, the teacher will continue to assess students' active monitoring, questioning, and repredicting as they read. Additionally, during the reading of social studies and other content material, students will be reminded that this kind of active thinking is also applicable to expository text.

Adapting This Example to Other Situations

This example assumes a middle school literature class. However, the strategy of monitoring, questioning, and repredicting is universal to all comprehension. Kindergarten teachers should also be teaching it. For instance, a kindergarten teacher might read the big book *Goodnight Moon*, by Margaret Wise Brown (Scholastic, 1947), to young students and talk about the active cycle of monitoring–questioning–repredicting.

Similarly, this strategy can be taught and used in conjunction with content materials such as science. For instance, a sixth-grade class using the textbook *AGS Physical Science* (American Guidance Service, 1997) would have an opportunity to monitor, question, and repredict in chapters such as the one on "Work and Machines" (pp. 181 ff.).

HOW WILL YOU KNOW THE LESSON HAS BEEN SUCCESSFUL?

In subsequent reading, students will be able to talk about the mental self-talk they did during reading. For instance, they will be able to describe where their monitoring caused them to pause and reconsider, the questions they posed for themselves as they read, and the occasions when they decided they needed to either modify a prediction or abandon it altogether and create a new one.

APPLICATION IN WRITING

Students become better writers if they think about how they read. For instance, maintaining coherence in writing is one of the most difficult things for young writers to do. However, students become more coherent writers when they apply to writing what they have learned in reading about monitoring, questioning, and repredicting. Specifically, being conscious of the monitoring–questioning–repredicting cycle of readers helps budding writers insert into their writing clues that help minimize the amount of questioning and repredicting their readers will have to do.

Imaging

Good readers respond to the descriptive text they read, especially when reading narrative text. They create pictures in their minds, or images. It is sometimes called "visualizing."

Like so much of comprehension, imaging is something good readers seem to do "naturally." To them, reading a book is like watching a movie: they see and hear what is happening as it transpires.

However, some readers have difficulty creating images of what they read. They do not understand how to use descriptive language to create "pictures in their minds" about what is happening.

Like all comprehension strategies, imaging requires readers to use prior knowledge and to predict. In this case, the prior knowledge the reader uses is experience with words and descriptive language. Readers use what that descriptive language makes them think to create an image. That is, they predict what image the author intends to convey. Because descriptive language appears with more frequency in narrative than in expository text, imagery tends to be taught in conjunction with stories rather than with textbooks or other informational texts.

Imagery is particularly important to reading narrative text because it is often the image that make stories vibrant and alive. Readers see what the characters see, hear what the characters hear, and feel what the characters feel. It is these emotional responses that often "hook" students and cause them to think that reading is "cool." Thus, if we can develop imaging, there is a good chance we can motivate students to make recreational reading a permanent part of their lives.

How Will You Know You Need to Teach Imaging?

The situation: Students listen to stories being read to them or read stories on their own but do not seem to be emotionally involved in what is happening.

The data you collect: Provide students with a piece of drawing paper and crayons, read a particularly descriptive passage to them, and ask them to draw what the text made them see. Or, similarly, read a particularly descriptive passage and ask students to tell you how it made them feel, or what they heard, or what they see in their minds. If the resulting descriptions are sparse, there may be a need to teach imaging.

Explaining the Forest as Well as the Trees

Big understandings you might need to explain when teaching imagery:

♦ That comprehension requires proactive effort.

♦ That authors want readers to see and hear and feel certain things, especially in the narrative text they write.

♦ That authors use descriptive language so we can use our senses of sight, hearing, smelling, feeling, and tasting to construct an image of what the author wants us to see or hear or feel or taste.

KEEPING THE MAIN THING THE MAIN THING

This example assumes a first-grade setting. A day earlier, the teacher had orally read Jane Yolen's *Owl Moon* (Scholastic, 1987) as part of a class project on "What makes stories fun?" Because the story has so much descriptive language, the teacher wants to use the same book today to develop the strategy of imaging. It is being taught as a listening comprehension strategy because these students have not yet learned to read well enough to read the book on their own.

The Student's Objective

By the end of this lesson, you will be able to tell what you see and hear and feel as you hearw stories like *Owl Moon*, and you will be able to tell what clues you used to figure out what you see or hear or feel.

What Is the "Secret" to Doing It?

Students must:

♦ Identify words the author is using that are descriptive.

♦ Use prior knowledge about those words and about our senses to create an image in the mind.

LESSON INTRODUCTION

Say something like:

"Yesterday I read *Owl Moon* to you and we really enjoyed learning about going owling. Today we are going to use *Owl Moon* again, but this time we are going to use it to learn a new listening strategy. This strategy is called 'imaging.' That means that I build pictures in my mind of what I am hearing so that I can see and hear and feel what is happening in the story. Sometimes I can even smell or taste what is happening. I'm going to show you how I build those pictures in my mind using the first few pages of *Owl Moon*. The secret to building these mind pictures is to think about the words the author uses to describe things and about what my experience with those words causes me to see or hear or feel (or maybe even smell or taste). Pay close attention because as we move through *Owl Moon*. I will be asking you to show me how *you* build pictures in your minds using the words you hear the author using."

MODELING THE THINKING

Say something like:

> "Let's reread the first page of *Owl Moon* so I can show you how I make images in my mind as I am reading. Right here on the first page it says, 'The trees stood still as giant statues.' Here's a place where the author is using words that describe. She is describing the trees. She says the trees were like 'giant statues.' The author is trying to get me to picture the trees the way she is seeing the trees. To see them that way, I have think about what I know about statues. I have experience with statues. I can picture in my mind what giant statues would look like—they'd be really big, and they wouldn't move at all because they are made out of stone. So that's what I would see in my mind. I could draw a picture of it.
>
> "Let's try another passage on the same page. The author says that 'Somewhere behind us a train whistle blew, long and low, like a sad, sad song.' Here the author is trying to get us to *hear* something, not *see* something. And she wants us to hear it like she hears it. To be able to hear the train whistle the way the author wants me to hear it, I have to think about what I know about the clues the author gives me. She says the train whistle is 'long and low, like a sad, sad song.' What I have to do is think about what I know about sad songs. When I think of sad songs, it seems like the music is all stretched out. So I think of sounds that are all stretched out. See how my experience with the clues the author provides can be used to hear and see what the author wants me to hear and see?"

SCAFFOLDED ASSISTANCE

Example 1: Extensive Teacher Help

Say something like:

> "Let's see if you can help me create the next image. On the next page the author says, 'A farm dog answered the train, and then a second dog joined in. They sang out, train and dogs, for a real long time.' Is the author trying to get us to see something here or

to hear something? Yes, she wants us to hear something like she hears it. What clues does the author give us? The two dogs who are 'singing out' with the train whistle are clues we can use. We have to think whether we have experience with dogs 'singing out.' Have you ever heard something like that? Okay, then you can use that experience to hear in your mind what the character in *Owl Moon* is hearing. What does it sound like?"

Example 2: Less Teacher Help

Say something like:

"If we go on to the next page, we find the author saying, 'Our feet crunched over the crisp snow. . . . ' Is the author trying to get you to create an image here? Yes, she may be trying to get us to hear it like she hears it. What are the clue words? Yes, 'crunched' is a clue and 'crisp' is a clue. Do you have experience with snow that 'crunched' and was 'crisp'? What did it sound like? If that's the way it sounded to you, that may be the way it sounded to the author too. So now you can hear it. But let's think more about 'crunched' and 'crisp.' Maybe the author is trying to get us to use more than just our sense of hearing. Maybe there's another sense we could use to create an image here. Have you ever experienced walking over snow that 'crunched'? Could you feel it as well as hear it? What did it feel like to you? Good. Do you think that maybe it feels that way to the author too? So we are both hearing and feeling when we listen to this section of the story."

Example 3: No Teacher Help

As students get better at creating images, move to other parts of the book and have them describe the images they are creating and the thinking they are doing to create those images.

APPLICATION IN READING

This is an example in which a strategy is developed after reading the text. But continued application will occur on subsequent days when the teacher orally reads different stories. In those situations, it will be important for students to continue creating images from the clues they hear. Eventually, of course, as these first graders begin reading, they will apply to their reading the image-building strategy they have been using in listening.

Adapting This Example to Other Situations

The above example is set in a first-grade listening situation. However, imaging can be taught at any grade level, and in reading as well as in listening. For instance, fifth or sixth graders reading Natalie Babbitt's *Tuck Everlasting* (Bantam Dell, 1975) will encounter passages such as the following that inspire image building:

> The road . . . wandered along in curves and easy angles, swayed off and up in a pleasant tangent to the top of a small hill, ambled down again between fringes of bee-hung clover, and then cut sidewise across a meadow.

As with the sample above, the "secret" is to use of the author's clues and your experience with words the author uses. In this case, for instance, experience with the words *wandering* and *pleasant* and *ambled* evoke a peaceful image.

HOW WILL YOU KNOW THE LESSON HAS BEEN SUCCESSFUL?

In subsequent listening situations, students should evidence greater emotional involvement in the stories. Students should give tangible evidence of excitement or sadness or scariness, depending on what is happening. Further, when asked, they should be able to describe verbally what they see and hear as they listen (or, for older students, when they read) and the thinking process they used to create the image.

APPLICATION IN WRITING

The relationship between reading and writing is particularly clear when teaching imaging. Students should apply their imaging strategy not only when listening and reading but also when composing their own stories. During those writing experiences, students should be encouraged to reverse the imaging process. Rather than thinking of imaging from the standpoint of a reader trying to figure out what an author is trying to get us to see or hear or feel, students should be encouraged to think about it as a writer trying to get a reader to see or hear or feel. The more students practice composing text that helps readers create images, the better they will be at creating images as readers.

EXAMPLE 8

Inferring

Inferring is the ability to "read between the lines" or to get the meaning an author implies but does not state directly. As noted in Chapter 2, virtually all comprehension strategies involve inferring in the sense that comprehension requires readers to note text clues, to access prior knowledge associated with those clues, and then, on the basis of that background knowledge, predict (or infer) what the meaning is. So, in this sense, inferring is something a reader does as part of all comprehension strategies.

Stated another way, comprehension always involves trying to "get inside the author's head" to see what he or she really meant when the text was composed. The reader, operating from one set of background experiences, cannot precisely know the mind of an author, who is operating from a different experience background. The reader must make a calculated guess as to an author's meaning. Even when an author says something straightforward, such as "The dress was red," the reader must infer the shade of red, the style of the dress, and so on. In this sense, virtually all comprehension requires inference, and students should learn from the very beginning that reading is a matter of actively *inferring* meaning, based on prior knowledge about text information.

While reading between the lines is part of all comprehension, it is nonetheless useful to teach inferring as a separate strategy, particularly in narrative text where readers often are expected to infer the traits of characters or to infer mood. Character traits are seldom stated explicitly but instead are implied by describing what a person does or says. Similarly, mood is seldom stated directly but instead is implied by describing the physical environment or the behavior of characters. It is up to the reader to infer the mood. The following example illustrates how one might teach this strategy.

How Will You Know You Need to Teach Inferring?

The situation: In discussing narrative text that has been read, you note that students cannot answer questions about character traits or mood or other information the author implies but does not state explicitly.

The data you collect: You can confirm that students need to learn inferring by asking them to listen to or read a narrative passage that contains clues to character traits or mood but does not state it explicitly. If students cannot use the clues to decide what is happening in sentences like these, they may need explanations about how to infer.

Explaining the Forest as Well as the Trees

Big understandings you might need to explain when teaching inferring:

♦ What we mean when we say meaning is "implied" or is "between the lines."

♦ That authors compose text based on their experience background and we construct meanings based on what the author's words make us think about (i.e., our experience background).

♦ That authors often leave information unstated or implied, expecting readers to infer it.

♦ That comprehension is an active process of *constructing* meaning, which means we must infer.

♦ That inferring is virtually the same process as predicting.

KEEPING THE MAIN THING THE MAIN THING

This example assumes a sixth-grade class. The teacher uses a reader's workshop structure, with the class divided into several literature circles. Each group is reading a different novel, and all the groups will come together at a later point to debate whether novels are "enriching." One group is reading E. L. Konigsburg's *The View from Saturday* (Scholastic, 1996). Because the teacher has noted that the members of this group sometimes have difficulty inferring, she decides to teach a specific lesson on how to infer and to have students apply the strategy when reading the next chapter in *The View from Saturday*.

The Student's Objective

By the end of this lesson, you will be able to state information E. L. Konigsburg has not directly stated but instead has inserted "between the lines" of *The View from Saturday*, and you will be able to describe the thinking you used to do it.

What Is the "Secret" to Doing It?

Students must:

♦ Note the clues embedded in the text.

♦ Access their own experience regarding these clues.

♦ Make predictions about the implied meaning based on their experience with the clues the author provides.

LESSON INTRODUCTION

Say something like:

"We have been reading *The View from Saturday*, and we are going to continue doing so today. But because I have noted that you need some help figuring out meaning an author is embedding in a story without really saying it, I want to first teach you a strategy for 'reading between the lines.' After I teach you how to do that, we'll then read the next chapter in *The View from Saturday*, and you will have an opportunity to use the strategy we learn today. The thing you have to pay attention to is how I use my own knowledge and experience with the clues the author provides to figure out what meaning the author is implying."

MODELING THE THINKING

Say something like:

"Let me show you how I figure out meaning that is not directly stated in the text by using an example like the following:

The sky was dark and the fog blocked out everything. I couldn't see three feet in front of me. I didn't know which way to turn. I was frozen to the spot.

"The author is implying something here about mood or feeling. But nothing in this text tells me directly about mood or feeling, but I can figure out how the character is feeling by putting myself in his place and using my own experience. What I do is say to myself, 'If it were me who was out on a dark and foggy night and didn't know which way to turn, how would that make me feel?' I would probably decide that in such a situation I would feel scared. If I would be scared in that situation, then probably that is how the character in the story feels too. So, to get information the author doesn't state directly, I use what the author tells me but I think about my own experience with it and make a prediction on the basis of my experience. In this case, I thought about how I would feel in that same situation and predicted that the author wanted me to feel like that."

SCAFFOLDED ASSISTANCE

Example 1: Extensive Teacher Help

Following the modeling, provide another example, and have students assist you as you continue to take the lead in teaching the strategy. The example might be something like this:

> When the teacher praised her for the good job she did, Mildred lowered her eyes and blushed. She said, "Oh, it was nothing. Anybody could have done it." When the teacher continued to praise her, Mildred got even more red in the face.

Then say something like:

> "Let's look at this example together. The author is implying something here about the kind of person Mildred is. So how are we going to figure out what the author wants us to think about Mildred? Does the author give us some clues? Yes, she says that, when praised, Mildred lowered her eyes, blushed, and then got even redder in the face. In order to use these clues to figure out what the author wants us to think, we have to think about our own experience with people like that. Have you ever known someone who, when praised, acts like Mildred did? So how would you describe that person? Yes, people who act like that sometimes are embarrassed. So because that is what our experience tells us about people who lower their eyes and blush, probably the author wants us to think that Mildred is embarrassed."

Example 2: Less Teacher Help

Say something like:

> "Now let's try another example, but this time I will not give you as much help. You must do more of the thinking yourselves, and I'm

just going to ask you questions to point you in the right direction. Remember the secret to doing this: first, look for clues the author provides, then think about your own experience with those clues, and, on the basis of your experience, predict what meaning the author is implying. Here's the example:

> The team boarded the school bus and started out for the big game. If they won this game, they would be champions! Suddenly, 15 miles from the site of the game, the bus broke down. There they sat, waiting. Nobody seemed to know what to do, and it was getting closer and closer to game time.

"In this example, the author doesn't tell you what the players are feeling. Instead, the author assumes you will figure it out for yourselves. So what do we do to figure out what the author is implying here? Are there clues? And can you think of experiences you have had that were similar in some way? How did you feel in those situations? If that is how you felt, can you predict how the team players in this example felt?"

Example 3: No Teacher Help

Once students demonstrate confidence in inferring, you might want to use an example from *The View from Saturday* but provide little or no assistance. For instance, you might say:

"Okay, now let's look at an example in the story we're reading in our literature circle. Read the first paragraph in Chapter 3, where the principal, Margaret Draper, is being described. Read the paragraph to yourselves. E. L. Konigsburg doesn't come right out and tell us what kind of principal Margaret Draper was, but she gives us clues and wants us to figure it out for ourselves. Look for those clues, and use your own experience to decide what kind of principal she was. Remember that I am going to ask you to tell me how you figured it out, so be aware of the thinking you are doing as you use the strategy."

APPLICATION IN READING

This example illustrates how to teach the strategy and then apply it to a text selection. The teacher will continue to monitor students' application as they read other chapters in *The View from Saturday*. For instance, immediately following the Chapter 3 example above, the author states that "Sixth graders had stopped asking 'Now what?' and had started asking 'So what?' " Deciding what Konigsburg is implying about sixth graders requires the use of inference.

Adapting This Example to Other Situations

Inferring should be taught at all grade levels and is applicable in listening situations as well as in reading situations. For instance, one could use the big book version of Tomie dePaola's *Mice Squeak, We Speak* (Scholastic, 1998). When reading this book orally to kindergartners, you could explain how to infer, using as examples the meaning dePaola wants the reader to get regarding what is really different about the noises animals make and the noises humans make. The secret remains the same: look for clues, use what you know about the clues, and then predict what the "hidden" meaning is.

HOW WILL YOU KNOW THE LESSON HAS BEEN SUCCESSFUL?

You will be able to determine that the lesson was a success if, after reading or listening to a story, students are able to answer questions that require comprehending what the author has implied but has not directly stated, and if students can describe the thinking they did to do such inferring.

APPLICATION IN WRITING

Students often understand inferring best if, during their own writing, they are encouraged to imply meaning. Consequently, when teaching children to infer during reading, it is often wise to also plan writing lessons in which students are encouraged to insert into their writing various kinds of implied meaning. Being metacognitive about how to imply meaning when writing is just as important as being metacognitive about how one infers meaning when reading, so students should be encouraged when writing to report what clues they are leaving for the reader and what meaning they expect the reader to infer from those clues.

EXAMPLE 9

Look-Backs as Fix-It Strategies

Blockages to meaning are not unusual while reading. The reader monitors meaning getting, but suddenly things don't make sense. Good readers learn that such instances are normal and that they call for problem-solving techniques. That is, the blockage poses a problem to be solved before proceeding. These problem-solving techniques are often called "fix-it strategies" or "fix-up strategies" because the reader "fixes" the situation so that meaning getting can continue. The context strategy described in Example 3, for instance, can be thought of as a "fix-it strategy."

Fix-it strategies are also frequently referred to as "look-backs." This is a somewhat misleading term. While it is true that, in order to remove a blockage, a reader often goes back and rereads the text, sometimes it is necessary to read ahead. Consequently, the term "look-backs" really refers to a strategy in which readers search backward and sometimes forward in a text to remove a meaning blockage encountered while reading. To use look-backs, readers first need to understand that it is essential to monitor meaning getting as you read and that good readers stop when a problem is encountered (see, e.g., Example 6).

The idea of stopping sometimes poses a problem because it seems to conflict with fluency (see Examples 22 and 23). Stopping to fix a blockage is a break in fluency. Consequently, teachers sometimes have difficulty deciding when to promote fluency and when to promote stopping to problem-solve. However, the problem is eased if we keep in mind that fluency should be developed using easy text in which the need to "fix" a problem is encountered relatively infrequently. The strategy of look-backs, in contrast, should be learned in situations where teachers and students are reading slightly more difficult text where problems are more likely to be encountered.

Once a reader stops and acknowledges that a problem exists, the next step is to decide what is causing the problem. Sometimes the problem is an unknown word meaning, and the reader solves the problem by reading backward (or forward) to find context clues to help figure out the meaning of the word (see Examples 3 and 21). Sometimes the problem involves changing predictions (see Example 5). Sometimes the problem requires making an inference (see Example 8). Consequently, as with virtually all comprehension, the key is prior knowledge, but in this case it is prior knowledge about previously learned strategies.

How Will You Know You Have to Teach Look-Backs?

The situation: Students keep on reading even when what they are reading no longer makes sense, or they stop at points when the text no longer makes sense but make no attempt to fix the problem.

The data you collect: If students keep reading even when the text no longer makes sense, they probably need instruction in monitoring (see Example 5). However, if they stop but do not attempt to fix the problem, ask them to talk to you about what they are thinking when they stop. If their responses indicate that they do not even try to remove the blockage or that they do not understand how to apply strategies to solve problems when reading, they may need instruction in look-backs.

Explaining the Forest as Well as the Trees

Big understandings you might need to explain when teaching fix-it strategies:

♦ That good readers stop reading when a problem is encountered.

♦ That strategies learned in other situations can be applied when meaning blocks are encountered.

♦ That previously learned strategies can be combined and learned together.

KEEPING THE MAIN THING THE MAIN THING

This example is situated in a fifth-grade unit on the Civil War. At the beginning of the unit, the teacher solicited from students questions they would like answered about the Civil War. She then categorized the questions, put students into groups based on the questions posed, and for each group identified an appropriate children's literature book having potential for answering questions in that category. The whole class will read about the Civil War using the social studies textbook but, in addition, each group reading a particular literature selection reflecting their particular category of questions will share what they found with the class. In the following example, a group interested in questions about slavery both before and during the Civil War is reading *Harriet Tubman and the Fight against Slavery,* by Bree Burns (Chelsea Juniors, 1992). The teacher uses the text as an opportunity to teach look-backs as a comprehension strategy.

The Student's Objective

By the end of this lesson, you will be able look back in the text or, sometimes, look forward in the text to solve a problem that blocked your meaning getting, and you will be able to describe the thinking you did to solve the problem.

What Is the "Secret" to Doing It?

Students must:

- Stop when the text stops making sense.
- Identify what is blocking the meaning.
- Think about what strategy they know that could be used to fix the problem.
- Apply the strategy.
- Test to see if the problem is fixed.

LESSON INTRODUCTION

Say something like:

"Your group asked a lot of questions about slavery before the Civil War and during the Civil War. To help you answer those questions, we are going to read *Harriet Tubman and the Fight against Slavery*. This is the biography of a woman who was a slave and who escaped and then spent many years helping other slaves to escape. In reading about the life of Harriet Tubman, you will answer many of the questions you had about slavery.

"But because this book is difficult in some places, you may encounter some problems as you are reading. So we are going to read the first chapter together, and I'm going to show you what good readers do when they run into problems while they are reading. The strategy is called 'look-backs' because, when good readers get stuck while reading, they look backward in the text (and sometimes they even read ahead) to fix the problem. Pay attention to the way I do this so you can do it yourselves as we read further in the chapter. There are four things I do once I realize I have a problem. First, I figure out what the problem is. Then I think about the strategies I have learned to see if one will help me here. Then I put the strategy to work. And then I test to see if the text now makes sense to me."

MODELING THE THINKING

Say something like:

> "Let me show you how I use the look-back strategy in Chapter 1. This chapter will answer one or two of the questions you have about slavery. But as you read you will find some difficult words. When that happens, you use the look-back strategy. For instance, let's read to the top of the second page [page 8]. When I start, everything is going smoothly. I am using my previously learned monitoring strategy, asking myself as I read, 'Does this make sense?' But suddenly at the end of the paragraph at the top of page 8, I run into the word *auction*, and that doesn't make sense to me. So the first thing I do is stop. Then I say to myself, 'What is the problem here? Why am I stuck?' I answer myself by saying that I am stuck on the word *auction*. I don't know what it means, so my meaning getting is blocked here. Then I survey the strategies I have learned. Do I know a strategy that will help me here? I remember that I have learned to use context clues to figure out unknown words. So I look back in the text to see if there are any clues to help me. I find that it says, ' . . . millions of men, women and children had been kidnapped from their homes in Africa and were sold on the auction block. . . . ' That helps me a little bit because the word *sold* is a clue. 'Auction block' has to have something to do with selling. But I'm still puzzled about exactly what it means. So I look ahead to see if there are clues. The sentence goes on to say, ' . . . like farm animals, to the highest bidder.' The words *to the highest bidder* help me understand 'auction.' It must mean selling something to people who make bids, with the highest bidder getting it. I check to see whether the sentence now makes sense. It does, so I can go on reading.
>
> "See how I identified the problem, thought about a strategy I could apply, put that to work, and then checked to see if it now makes sense? This is what we are learning to do today. Let's see if we can do an example together."

SCAFFOLDED ASSISTANCE

Example 1: Extensive Teacher Help

Say something like:

> "Let's use the sentences under the picture on page 9 as an example
> and do it together. Let's read those sentences. When I read it and
> monitor my meaning getting, it makes sense in the first line and
> in the second line. But do you find something in the third line
> that you don't know? Yes, I don't know what 'middle passage' is
> either. So we have to stop because we are questioning what this
> is. So what's the problem? Why did we stop? What is blocking our
> meaning getting? The blockage is the words *middle passage*. So
> we have to think to ourselves, 'Do we know a strategy we could
> use here?' and, like the model I just did for you, we could use
> our context strategy. So let's look back. Reread the first two lines.
> There is a context clue to what 'middle passage' is. Yes, it says that
> 'across the Atlantic Ocean' was 'known as' the middle passage.
> So what must the middle passage be? Yes, it must be the Atlantic
> Ocean. Now let's read it and see if 'middle passage' makes sense.
> Does it? Yes, so we can go on reading."

Example 2: Less Teacher Help

Say something like:

> "Let's read on. Tell me the first time you come to a problem. What
> is the first problem you find? Okay, in the middle paragraph on
> page 11, you stopped at the word *bondage* because you were mon-
> itoring and it stopped making sense when you ran into that word.
> That's a hard one to figure out, but let's apply our look-back strat-
> egy and see if we can fix it. First, we have to identify the problem.
> What is the problem? Yes, it's a word we don't know. So now we
> have to think about whether we know anything that would help
> us solve that problem. Do we have a strategy? Yes, just as before,
> we can use our context strategy to figure out words we don't know.
> So first look back and see if there are context clues you can use.
> Yes, the word *slaves* and *escape* are clues. By thinking what it is
> that slaves try to escape, maybe 'bondage' means the same thing

as 'slavery.' Let's test it out. Does that make sense there? Yes, so we can read on."

Example 3: No Teacher Help

If students are responding well, you might have them read on and report when they run into a blockage that needs to be fixed. You would expect such a report when they encounter the word *abolitionist* on page 13. If they are using the strategy well, students will report that they identified the problem as a word meaning blockage, that they thought about using context, that they found no context clues when they looked back but they found some when they looked ahead, and that once they identified an abolitionist as someone who wants to end slavery, the problem was fixed and they could read on.

APPLICATION IN READING

This example illustrates how a strategy can be taught while the selection is being read. Students will continue to use their look-back strategy as they read *Harriet Tubman*. But the teacher will also ensure that students are using look-backs when reading their social studies text, their recreational reading books, and so on.

Adapting This Example to Other Situations

This example assumes a fifth grade using a biography in conjunction with a social studies unit on the Civil War. However, the strategy of look-backs can be used at various grade levels, in various kinds of text, and can employ various kinds of strategies in addition to context clues. For instance, in a first-grade class where the teacher is reading the big book *Humphrey the Wrong-Way Whale*, by Gare Thompson (Scholastic, 1989), the strategy of look-backs could be used on pages 4 and 5 to help the listening children keep oriented about what is happening to Humphrey. For instance, the teacher might stop after page 5 and say something like, "I'm a little confused about what's happening to Humphrey here. When good readers get confused, they stop and look back. Let's stop here, look back, and see if we are sure about what is happening to Humphrey."

HOW WILL YOU KNOW THE LESSON HAS BEEN SUCCESSFUL?

You will know the lesson has been successful if, during conversations with students about their reading, they report instances in which they have encountered meaning blockages while reading and are able to describe the thinking process they used to repair the blockage so they could go on reading.

APPLICATION IN WRITING

The analogous writing application is revision. Good writers frequently "look back" on what they have written and when necessary revise. Students are aided in the use of look-backs in reading (and in writing) if they are encouraged to keep the reader in mind while writing, revising when necessary to minimize the number of blockages the reader might encounter when the composed text is read.

EXAMPLE 10

Main Idea

Main idea refers to the "big idea" or the most important idea found in expository text. Narratives also have a "big idea" but we call it a "theme" (see Example 11).

"Main idea" is often confused with "topic." In a book about locomotives, for instance, the topic may be "locomotives," but the main idea is what the author wants readers to understand is important about locomotives. While it is relatively easy to identify topic, it is harder to determine what the author thinks is important.

The main idea is very difficult to teach for four reasons. First, while the main idea is sometimes contained in a topic sentence of a paragraph, most expository text main ideas, as well as most themes in stories, are implied by the author rather than stated explicitly. Second, main idea is difficult because the reader must look across several pages of text and, using the sum of the information provided and prior knowledge, predict the underlying message. Third, determining main idea is difficult to do because we seldom know for sure what an author's main idea is, or whether the author might have more than one main idea. The reader's analysis can only be a "best prediction." Finally, main idea thinking is difficult because it is tentative. Readers often have to alter main ideas when new information is encountered later in the text.

To determine the main idea, readers must understand that authors write because they have some important ideas to convey. Consequently, determining the main idea means readers must question where the author is placing value, or emphasis.

While main idea is difficult to teach, the good news is that the thinking process is basically the same as for other comprehension strategies. That is, the reader uses text clues, accesses background knowledge triggered by those clues and, based on that background knowledge, predicts what the author thinks is most important. What makes it difficult is that the reader must look for clues across several pages of text and combine together the predictions about what is important.

How Will You Know You Need to Teach Recognizing the Main Idea?

The situation: Students cannot correctly answer questions about what the author wants readers to think is most important.

The data you collect: Give students paragraphs to read such as the following:

> Because their school only had a boys' team, the girls got together and formed a soccer team of their own. They scheduled games with both girls' teams and boys' teams. They won almost every game they played. They even beat the boys' team at their own school!

If students cannot state the most important idea—or main idea—in listening or reading situations such as these, they may benefit from explanations about how to determine the main idea.

Explaining the Forest as Well as the Trees

Big understandings you might need to explain when teaching the main idea:

- ♦ That authors have a purpose for writing that reflects what they think is important.
- ♦ That the author's topic and the author's most important idea are not necessarily the same.
- ♦ That questioning as one reads is particularly essential.

- ♦ That not everything in a text is equally important.
- ♦ That determining the main idea is like predicting, but that the predictions we make about the main idea early in the text must be combined together with what we predict is most important at the end of the text.

KEEPING THE MAIN THING THE MAIN THING

This example is set in a third grade. The class is studying flowers in science. Because the teacher wants her students to use literacy to take action on important issues, the study of flowers has been approached from the perspective of what the third-grade class could do to promote the preservation of flowers. Yesterday the teacher introduced the expository text *Meadow: A Close-Up Look at the Natural World of a Meadow*, by Barbara Taylor (Dorling Kindersley, 1992), and she and the class discussed how they might use the book as a way to decide what they can do to preserve flowers in nature. Today, the teacher returns to the book, using it as an opportunity to teach students a strategy for determining the main idea in an expository text.

The Student's Objective

By the end of this lesson, you will be able to state the most important thing an author is telling you, and you will be able to describe the thinking you did to decide what was most important.

What Is the "Secret" to Doing It?

Students must:

- ♦ Put themselves in the place of the author.
- ♦ Identify words and phrases (the details) that might be clues to what is important.
- ♦ Use those details to make a prediction about what is important by asking questions about what, in their

experience, the clues seem to say about what the author thinks is most important.

♦ Combine predictions made early in the text with predictions made later in the text.

♦ Ultimately decide what the main idea is by saying, "If I had written this and said things this way, what would that say about what I thought was important?"

LESSON INTRODUCTION

Say something like:

"Yesterday we began looking at this book on meadows, and we discussed how we might use the information to help us decide what we can do to preserve flowers in nature. Today we are going to return to this book so that I can show you a strategy that will help us decide what the author wants us to get as the most important point. The strategy I want to show you is called 'main idea.' Determining importance is hard to do for two reasons. First, authors seldom come right out and say what they think is important. Instead, they expect us to figure out for ourselves what they think is important. Second, to figure out the main idea we must look at several clues over several pages and decide how they go together. Let me show you a strategy you can use to figure out what the main idea is. I use this strategy during reading and after reading because I'm always thinking about what is most important about what I just read. The secret is to put yourself in the author's place, look for clues the author provides, and then try to think of those clues in combination to decide how they go together. Let me show you. Pay attention to what I do because when I get done I'm going to ask you to do what I did."

MODELING THE THINKING

Say something like:

> "Let's look at the first chapter on page 8. Yesterday we read it together. But good readers return to the text after reading and think about what the author wants us to understand is most important. To decide that, I first have to 'get inside the author's head' or put myself in the author's place to decide what the author considers important. So I reread the first four sentences and try to decide what the author is thinking. The author here is Barbara Taylor, and she provides details such as the meadow is full of 'colorful flowers' and is 'buzzing with insects' and is 'home' to many animals. These are clues to what she thinks is important. When I combine these clues and use my own experience to decide what all these words have in common, all the words seem to convey a good feeling. So I predict that the author is trying to make the meadow sound like a good place. That seems to be a main idea— until I come to the next two sentences. They say 'many meadows have been plowed over' and that 'wildlife finds it hard to survive.' So now I have to combine those ideas that sound bad with what came before that sounded good. I have to think to myself, 'Why did the author combine these two things?' To help me answer that, I put myself in the author's place and say to myself, 'If I was the author and I thought meadows were good, how would I feel if they were plowed over and if wildlife could no longer survive? I would not be happy about that.' So I predict that the author's most important idea in this chapter is that we should not plow over meadows because it destroys the good things in meadows.
>
> "Did you see how I 'read between the lines' to find clues, combined the clues together, and tried to put myself in the author's place to decide the author's most important idea?"

SCAFFOLDED ASSISTANCE

Example 1: Extensive Teacher Help

Say something like:

> "Let's try another example from Barbara Taylor's book, but this time you have to help me. Let's look at Chapter 3, on 'Flower Power.' We read this yesterday, but now we are going back into the text to decide on what the main idea is. We have to pretend that we are the author and that we have used certain words because, in combination, they give the reader clues to what we think is most important. For instance, look at the chapter title. If you were the author, why would you choose the title 'Flower Power'? What does your experience tell you about those words? Yes, when we've heard phrases like that in the past, they usually meant that something was powerful. So, maybe the author is saying flowers are powerful. Let's read on and continue to think about the details the author is providing and what our experience makes us think about those clues in combination. The text says that plants, especially wild flowers that are sometimes called 'weeds,' do lots of things. Do the words make us think they are good things? Yes, the author says these plants are 'attractive' and that they provide 'food and shelter for many creatures.' When combined together, they seem to suggest something good. So the author's main idea here must be a positive one. Think to yourself: if you were the author and you were saying these things, what would be the important idea you were trying to convey? Yes, it seems sensible to say that the important idea here is that meadow plants are important. Can you describe your thinking? Yes, you found clues the author used, you combined them together, and then you put yourself in the author's place to try to figure out what those clues together suggest might be the main idea."

Example 2: Less Teacher Help

Say something like:

> "Let's see if you can figure out the main idea when I give you less help. Look at the paragraph on page 13 called 'Late Developers.'

Let's see if we can use our strategy to figure out the main idea in this paragraph. We must pretend that we are the author, and we must ask ourselves, 'If I put in this combination of details, what would I be thinking is most important?' So what are the details? Yes, one detail is that insects spread the pollen for the flowers. Another is that flowers provide food for the insects. So I have to think about why I would say it this way if I were the author. In combination, it says insects do something for flowers, and flowers do something for insects. Taken together, what does that say about insects and flowers in a meadow? Yes, it sounds like the author is saying that insects and flowers depend on each other. Does that make sense as a main idea here?"

Example 3: No Teacher Help

When you observe that students are comfortable with the strategy, have them read another section of the book on meadows, figure out the main idea, and report the thinking they did to determine what was important.

APPLICATION IN READING

This example illustrates how a strategy can be taught following the reading of a selection. Continued application will occur as the class reads other books on flowers. Also, the teacher should ensure that students apply their main idea strategy to other content areas such as social studies.

Adapting This Example to Other Situations

This example has assumed a third-grade situation involving expository text. However, main idea strategies should be used at all grade levels and in various kinds of expository text. For instance, seventh graders studying Australia might use the book *Unique Animals and Birds of Australia* by Michael Morcombe (Lansdowne Press, 1973). The "secret" to the thinking process remains basically the same. The readers put themselves in the place of the author, think about the details in the scenes, and predict what the important message is. Similarly, the main idea can be taught when using content-area textbooks such as *World Geography* (Glencoe, 1987). When reading about the earth's structure (pp. 29 ff.), for instance, middle school students can use main idea thinking to determine what is most important in the discussion about the Earth's internal and external forces.

HOW WILL YOU KNOW THE LESSON HAS BEEN SUCCESSFUL?

This lesson will have been successful if, in future readings of expository text, the students can determine the main idea and can describe the thinking they did to identify what was important.

APPLICATION IN WRITING

Main idea thinking is as important in composing text as it is in comprehending text. To be a good writer, one must be able to compose coherent and cohesive text that keeps the reader "on track" and makes clear what the author thinks is important. Consequently, it is important for students to do lots of writing of expository text in which the goal is to convey clearly a main idea. Students will become better at reading for main idea (as well as better at composing coherent text) when main idea thinking is applied in writing as well as in reading.

EXAMPLE 11

Theme

While main idea is the "big idea" in expository text, *theme* is the big idea in narrative text. When authors write stories or poems or plays, they almost always have a message to convey about life, living, or humanity. Often, the theme is thought of as "the moral of the story," with *Aesop's Fables* being prominent examples of explicitly stated themes. More typically, however, a narrative's theme is implied rather than stated explicitly.

Like main idea, it is often difficult to identify the theme of a narrative. The reader must think across the text as a whole to figure it out.

But while theme is difficult, it is crucially important if students are to learn to appreciate literature. While narratives can be read purely for enjoyment, the best literature endures because it conveys a lasting message. Readers who understand that important things can be learned by reading narratives, and who have a strategy for identifying what the theme is, are prepared not only to enjoy literature but to profit from it.

While we often think of theme in association with mature literature and upper-grade literature classes, literature for young children also often has a theme. Think, for instance, of fairy tales, or Dr. Seuss stories, or of the Winnie the Pooh stories. They endure not only because they are fun to read but also because they have important messages to convey. Consequently, theme is not something to reserve for older students; it can be developed even with primary-grade children.

Like main idea, one determines theme by engaging in a two-step process of (1) questioning the author in a search for clues about what the theme may be and (2) reasoning about how the clues go together to convey a theme.

How Will You Know You Need to Teach Theme?

The situation: Students cannot discuss the important messages found in stories or poems, or show no evidence of understanding that narratives convey messages that go beyond the story line itself.

The data you collect: Read stories or poems to students and engage them in discussion of what we learn about people or life or living. If they cannot discuss such ideas, they may benefit from explanations about how to determine theme.

Explaining the Forest as Well as the Trees

Big understandings you might need to explain when teaching theme:

- ♦ That stories and poems can be read for fun, but that authors of stories and poems also have "big ideas" or "themes" they want to convey about life and living.
- ♦ That to determine theme, readers must engage in proactive questioning of the author.
- ♦ That theme is an *interpretation* based on one's experience background; therefore, different people may see different themes in a particular story or poem.
- ♦ That ideas can be combined together, or categorized, and the categories can be labeled as "subthemes" which in turn can be combined into a main "theme."

KEEPING THE MAIN THING THE MAIN THING

This example is set in a fifth grade. The teacher has partnered each of her fifth graders with a younger "buddy" in the school. The task is to write stories for their buddies that contain a message, or a theme. The fifth graders will then read those stories to their buddies and ultimately give them the stories for their classroom library. To prepare for developing the idea of theme, the teacher has just finished orally reading to the class Tom Birdseye's *Just Call Me Stupid* (Holiday House, 1993). Because theme is usually developed after reading, the teacher is now taking the students back through the story to model a strategy for figuring out theme.

The Student's Objective

By the end of this lesson, you will be able to state a theme for the story we just finished reading, and you will be able to describe the thinking you did to determine the theme.

What Is the "Secret" to Doing It?

Students must:

- ♦ Put themselves in the place of the main character in the story.
- ♦ Note the author's use of descriptive language for clues to how the character is feeling or thinking.
- ♦ Ask themselves questions about what, in their own experience, the clues about the character and about what is happening to the character make them think or feel in each part of the story.
- ♦ List what the clues make them feel or think for each part of the story (i.e., list the subthemes for each part of the story).
- ♦ Combine the subthemes and ask themselves, "What do these subthemes together seem to say about what message the author may be trying to convey?"

LESSON INTRODUCTION

Say something like:

> "We just finished reading *Just Call Me Stupid*. It was a great story.
> But the author was also trying to convey a 'big idea.' When you
> write stories for your buddies, you too will tell a story but you
> will also try to include in the story a big idea about living and life.
> We call those big ideas 'themes.' It is difficult to identify themes
> because we have to look across the story parts for 'little themes'
> or 'subthemes' and then combine those 'little themes' together to
> determine a big theme for the whole story. I'm going to show you
> how I do this in the first sections of the book and then you will do
> it with the later sections of the book."

MODELING THE THINKING

Say something like:

> "Let's look at Chapter 1. In the very first paragraph, Patrick is
> being scolded by his teacher because, even though he's a fifth
> grader, he doesn't know how to read. In the rest of the chapter,
> I learn that Patrick thinks he's stupid because he can't read. So
> I use this information to decide, based on my experience, how I
> would feel in this situation. I think Patrick must be feeling ter-
> rible about himself. So that's one 'subtheme.' Now I read on to
> Chapter 2 and find out that Patrick's father, who doesn't live with
> him anymore, calls him stupid even though his mother seems to
> believe in him. So again I think about how I would feel or what
> I would think. I think I'd feel like lots of people think I'm dumb,
> even if my mom doesn't. So that's a second 'subtheme.' Now I
> need to combine these two subthemes as ask myself, 'What do
> these two subthemes seem to be saying about what the author
> wants me to think?' When I look at these two subthemes together,
> it seems that the big idea the author is conveying is that you can
> feel bad about yourself if you can't read and the people around
> you do not all support you.

"Did you see how I used the author's clues and my experience with those feelings to make a prediction about what the 'subthemes' might be, and then how I combined those to make a big theme? Now let's see if we can do the same thing together for later sections of the story."

SCAFFOLDED ASSISTANCE

Example 1: Extensive Teacher Help

Say something like:

"Now let's look at Chapters 3 and 4, but now you have to help me figure out what the subthemes are and to combine them together into a big theme. In Chapter 3, we find that Patrick has created a 'kingdom' in his backyard. What does your experience tell you about why Patrick does that and how it makes him feel? Yes, probably Patrick is trying to find a place where he can feel good about himself. So the 'subtheme' for Chapter 3 would be that there is one place where Patrick feels good about himself. Now let's look at Chapter 4. What happens in Chapter 4 and how can you use your experience to figure out what the author is telling you about Patrick in this chapter? Yes, he's getting picked on at school but he makes himself feel better by drawing. So what does your experience cause you to predict about Patrick at this point. Yes, there's another place where Patrick feels good about himself and it's when he's drawing. So now let's look at these two subthemes. If we combine them together, we find that even though Patrick can't read, he does find ways to feel good about himself. So the big theme in Chapters 3 and 4 are that Patrick has ways of making himself feel good even though he can't read well."

Example 2: Less Teacher Help

Say something like:

"Let's see if you can figure out the subthemes in the next two chapters when I give you less help. Look at Chapters 5 and 6. What is happening in Chapter 5 and what does your experience tell you might be the subtheme here? Yes, Patrick finds a friend and he plays chess. So the subtheme is that Patrick can't be stupid because he plays chess. Now let's look at Chapter 6. Yes, in Chapter 6 we find that Patrick's friend helps him feel good about his ability to play chess and to draw. So what is the subtheme in Chapter 6? Yes, it's that his friend points out his strong points. Now combine those two subthemes. What is the big theme here? Yes, it is important that Patrick has a friend who recognizes that he is smart. So you used your experience with the clues the author provides in Chapter 5 and 6 to combine the two subthemes into a single big idea."

Example 3: No Teacher Help

The students continue going through the story chapter by chapter, developing the subthemes and the big themes with little help. Ultimately, they combine all the subthemes together and develop the overall theme of the book—that success is often tied to having a good friend who believes in you and helps you believe in yourself.

APPLICATION IN READING

Because determining theme usually occurs after having read a narrative, this example illustrates how a strategy can be taught following the reading of a selection. On subsequent days, the teacher will use other stories and poems and a similar strategy to help students figure out themes.

Adapting This Example to Other Situations

This example assumed a fifth-grade situation. However, themes can be developed in narratives at all levels. Consider, for instance, *Just Not Quite Right*, by Susan Ulrich Olsen (Mindset Press, 2000). A second-grade teacher could use this picture book, and the strategy described above, to identify theme. In this story about a near-sighted eagle who cannot hunt, the theme that develops across the story line is that handicaps do not limit what you can do.

How Will You Know the Lesson Has Been Successful?

You will know this lesson has been successful if, when discussing narratives on subsequent days, the students engage in discussion about the subthemes and the combination of sub-themes in big themes.

APPLICATION IN WRITING

Students are better able to identify theme when they also have experience in writing their own stories that include a theme. The fifth graders in this example are a good illustration. By writing their own stories for their "buddies" in the lower grades, they will become better at both interpreting theme in the stories they read and in writing stories of their own containing theme.

EXAMPLE 12

Summarizing

Summarizing is the creation of a brief retelling of a text. While it may include the main idea or theme, the focus is on describing in brief form the text's major points.

Primary-grade students often have difficulty summarizing because they want to tell everything. However, even middle school students sometimes have difficulty deciding what information to include in a summary and what not to include.

The best way to teach students to summarize is to teach them to organize their summaries around text structure. Well-written text is always well organized. That is, it has an internal structure. If readers have been taught to recognize the structure of a text, they can use it when summarizing.

Stories, for instance, have a structure that can be predicted or mapped. Some people teach students a "story map." A story map begins with a description of the characters, the setting, and the problem, then describes a series of events, and concludes with a resolution of the problem. Story maps that graphically display structure can be used to cue students to the internal structure of a story.

Expository text also is structured or mapped, but there are a variety of expository text structures. The most prevalent one is a variation on the old adage "Tell 'em what you're going to tell 'em, tell 'em, and then tell 'em what you told 'em"—that is, introduce the topic, state the facts one after another, then conclude. Other expository text structures include compare–contrast structures, chronological structures, and cause–effect structures, among others.

The following example illustrates how to explain using story structure to summarize narratives. It can be adapted to expository text by using the text structure as a guide to summarizing.

How Will You Know You Need to Teach Summarizing?

The situation: When you ask students to "tell you about" a story or a piece of expository text, they recite virtually everything that happened or report unimportant information and omit important information.

The data you collect: Ask students to provide a brief summary of a common fairy tale or a movie they saw. If they cannot be brief, or cannot identify the important information, they may profit from an explanation of how to summarize.

Explaining the Forest as Well as the Trees

Big understandings you may need to explain when teaching summarizing:

- The meaning of "beginning," "middle," and "end."
- That some information in text is more important than other information.
- That well-written texts have structure, and that looking for text structure will help them summarize.
- How to identify text structures in stories and in expository text.

KEEPING THE MAIN THING THE MAIN THING

This example is situated in a second-grade classroom. The teacher's major goal is to instill in her students a passion for recreational reading. Consequently she provides lots of time for "free reading" during the school day, has students read books of their choice for seat work when she is teaching a small group, and generally ensures that her students are engaged in reading stories of their choice for at least 60 minutes every school day. In addition, she provides multiple opportunities for students to share books they are reading in what she calls "Reader's Chair," a variation on the "Author's Chair" idea—that is, a student sits in a chair in a central location with fellow students gathered around and, instead of reading a self-composed story, he or she shares a favorite book. The teacher has noted that students' retellings often drag on too long because they do not know how to summarize. In this lesson, she uses Eva Bunting's *The Wall* (Clarion Books, 1990) to explain how story structure can be used to summarize books.

The Student's Objective

By the end of this lesson, you will be able to provide a short summary of a book you have read, and you will be able to describe how you used your knowledge of story structures to create the summary.

What Is the "Secret" to Doing It?

Students must:

- ◆ Understand the concepts of beginning, middle, and end.
- ◆ Know the parts of a story (story structure, or story map).
- ◆ Review the book to identify the parts of the story.
- ◆ Include just those parts in the summary.

LESSON INTRODUCTION

Say something like:

> "You have all enjoyed sharing favorite books during 'Reader's Chair.' But sometimes the sharing takes so long that we run out of time, and other students do not get a chance to share. So today I'm going to show you a strategy you can use to share your books more quickly. When we tell about our books briefly, we are providing a 'summary.' Instead of telling everything that happened in a story, a summary is a retelling of just the important parts of a story. The secret to making a summary is to think about story parts and to include just that information. Let me show you how I do it, and then we will use some of your books to try it out."

MODELING THE THINKING

Say something like:

> "I have just finished reading this book called *The Wall*. To get ready to share it during 'Reader's Chair,' I must do some planning so that my sharing does not take too long. To help me do that, I use a story map. A story map is like a picture of the major parts of a story. By using a story map as a guide, I tell only the important things that happened in the story. Here's what a story map looks like:

Beginning
- Who are the characters?
- Where is the story happening?
- What is the problem?

Middle
- What two or three things happened as the characters tried to solve the problem?

End
- How was the problem solved in the end?

"Let me show you how I use a story map to make a summary of *The Wall*. First, I look at the beginning to find out who the characters are, where the story is happening, and what the problem is. Right here on the first page, I find out that the characters in the story are a boy and his dad. The story is happening at a wall, and by using my prior knowledge and the clues from the picture, I can predict that it is the Vietnam Memorial. And it says the problem is to find grandfather's name on the wall. So now I have the first part of my summary. I can start by saying, 'This is a story of a boy and his dad. They are looking for the grandfather's name on the Vietnam Memorial.' In just two sentences I have summarized the beginning.

"Now I look at the middle of the book. The story map tells me I should tell just two or three things that happened in the middle as the boy and his dad try to find the grandfather's name. I can't tell everything, so I have to decide on which two or three things would be most helpful to my audience when I share the book. One thing that seems important is that lots of other people are there too. Another thing that seems important is that when they find Grandfather's name they rub a pencil lead sideways over a sheet of paper so that the name shows. And a third thing that seems important is that dad stands at the wall for a long time, even after all the school girls are there. So those are three things I can put in my summary for the middle of the story.

"Then I have to think about the end of the story. How was the problem solved in the end? They found Grandfather's name, and they put a picture of the boy by the wall. But the boy ends up thinking that he would rather have his grandfather with him.

"So, now I have a summary of the story that I can tell when I am sharing it in 'Reader's Chair.' Here's my summary:

A boy and his father were at the Vietnam Memorial. They were looking for Grandfather's name on the wall. There were lots of other people there. When they found the name, they rubbed a piece of paper over it so Grandfather's name showed through and they left a picture of the boy at the memorial. But Dad was sad and stood at the wall for a long time. In the end they found Grandfather's name, but the boy thought he'd rather have his grandfather with him.

"See how I used the story map to make a summary? I used the story map to help me decide what is most important to tell so that I would not take a lot of time during 'Reader's Chair.' Now let's see if you can do it."

SCAFFOLDED ASSISTANCE

Example 1: Extensive Teacher Help

Say something like:

"For the first try, Sarah and I will use the book she has just finished reading. We will do the thinking together out loud, and I will provide lots of help. Sarah, we are going to use the story map to guide our thinking as we decide on a summary. Let's look at the beginning of your story. Here are the two main characters. Here is where it is happening. Here is the problem. So we have the beginning of our summary. Now let's look at the middle. Let's see what happens. We have this happening, and this, and this, and this. We need to decide which two or three of those things we will include in our summary. We don't include everything because a summary is only the most important things that happen. You decide what's important by thinking what would be most helpful to you if you were listening to a summary of this book. Have you picked two or three things that would be important for the listeners to hear? Good. Now let's look at the ending. Did the problem get solved in the end? What will you say about how the problem was solved and how the story ended? Good. Now, take what we found at the beginning, the two or three things you decided were important from the middle, and what you have from the end and put them together. Can you say those things together? Tell me what your summary will say, and I will write it up here on the chart."

Example 2: Less Teacher Help

Say something like:

"Now let's try another one, but I will provide less help. Rodrigo, let's do your book. We'll use the story map to guide us. What do you need to do first? Yes, we need to look at the beginning. What do you find for characters, setting, and problem? Good. What do we do next? Okay, look in the middle of the book, and decide what two or three things you think are most important to include in your summary. And then what? Yes, we need to look at the end. What can you say to end your summary? Good. Put it all together and you have a good summary."

Example 3: No Teacher Help

When students can create a summary with little help, provide no assistance as others try it unless you observe students having difficulty.

APPLICATION IN READING

This example illustrates a strategy that is taught while using a story. The application would continue during subsequent "Reader's Chair" occasions. However, the teacher will also look for opportunities to have students apply their knowledge of story structure to summarize other narratives, such as movies kids have seen, books the teacher reads to them, and so on.

Adapting This Example to Other Situations

This example is set in a second grade and focuses on narrative text. However, summarizing should also be taught at other grade levels and in expository text. For instance, a fifth-grade teacher who has his class reading *A Dog's Gotta Do What a Dog's Gotta Do*, by Marilyn Singer (Holt, 2000), can use it to teach students how to summarize expository text. Chapter 2, for instance, is a good example of expository text that is organized on the standard "introduction, first fact, second fact, third fact, conclusion" kind of structure. The teacher can make a map of this structure (similar to a story map) and provide an explanation similar to the one for narrative text earlier in this example. The secret remains basically the same, but instead of story elements the focus is on topic, on subsequent pieces of factual information, and on the conclusion. By creating a statement for each part based on this structure, and then putting these

> statements together, a brief summary results. This also works very well in many social studies and science textbooks. For instance, the chapters in the middle school textbook titled *The Pacific Northwest: Past, Present and Future* (Directed Media, 1993) can be summarized using the same kind of expository text structure.

HOW WILL YOU KNOW THE LESSON HAS BEEN SUCCESSFUL?

You will know this lesson has been successful if, when asked to provide a brief summary of a story, students include the beginning, middle, and end components of a story and can describe how they used story structure to create their summaries.

APPLICATION IN WRITING

When students write stories, they should plan and draft them with a story map in mind. That is, the beginning should include the characters, the setting, and the problem; the middle should include important information about the problem; and the ending should be a resolution of the problem. Similarly, when students write expository text, they should utilize a structure. The more experience students have using text structures in their writing, the more they will be able to use text structures to summarize texts they have read.

Drawing Conclusions

Drawing conclusions is just another example of inferring that in turn is just another example of predicting. An author seldom states directly what a reader should conclude. More typically, a conclusion is implied. Consequently, drawing conclusions, like predicting and inferring, requires readers to be proactive in looking for clues in the text, thinking about what those clues trigger in prior knowledge, and making a prediction about what the author wants us to conclude on the basis of what makes sense in terms of past experience.

As with so many comprehension strategies, drawing conclusions is another example of the questioning good comprehenders do as they read. That is, when reading a text, readers ask themselves what the author wants them to be thinking at that point.

Readers should draw conclusions when reading both narrative and expository text, and the strategy can be taught in both listening and reading situations, whatever the grade level.

How Will You Know You Need
to Teach Drawing Conclusions?

The situation: Students are unable to answer questions such as "What does the author want you to be thinking in that section of the text?" or, with older students, "What conclusion can you draw from this text?"

The data you collect: To determine whether students need to learn how to draw conclusions, ask them to read or listen to a passage such as the following:

> Plants grow outdoors when there is a lot of sunlight and rain. We seldom see plants growing outdoors in January.

If students cannot draw a conclusion about what the author expects readers to conclude regarding why plants do not grow outdoors in January, they may profit from explanations about how to draw conclusions.

Explaining the Forest as Well as the Trees

Big understandings you might need to explain when teaching drawing conclusions:

- That authors often want readers to draw conclusions, even though they may not say so explicitly or do not specify exactly what conclusion should be drawn.
- That readers must be assertive *creators* of meaning.
- That drawing a conclusion is a prediction about what the author wants the reader to conclude.
- That like main idea and other comprehension strategies, the reader must pretend to be the author and, on that basis, think what conclusion the author might draw.

KEEPING THE MAIN THING THE MAIN THING

This example is set in a middle school. In an advanced English class, eighth graders are using the literature anthology titled *Themes in World Literature*, edited by George Elliott, Philip McFarland, Harvey Granite, and Morse Peckham (Houghton Mifflin, 1989), to read selections that build understandings about the role fate plays in the human condition. Yesterday students read two poems (Robert Frost's "The Road Not Taken," p. 313, and William Butler Yeats's "An Irish Airman Foresees His Death," p. 332) and discussed whether individual choice or the vagaries of fate are most influential in human life. Today the teacher wants to return to these two poems and use them to teach the strategy of drawing conclusions.

The Student's Objective

By the end of this lesson, you will be able to figure out what conclusion an author wants you to draw (even though it may not be stated), and you will be able to describe the thinking you did to draw the conclusion.

What Is the "Secret" to Doing It?

Students must:

♦ Think about the topic being discussed and ask what the author wants readers to think.

♦ Use experience about clue words to predict a conclusion.

♦ Put themselves in the author's shoes and ask, " Why would I say what is being said here if I were the author?"

LESSON INTRODUCTION

Say something like:

"Yesterday, we read both 'The Road Not Taken' and 'An Irish Airman Foresees His Death,' and we discussed them in terms of our goal of understanding whether humans really control their destiny or are victims of fate. We tentatively decided that Frost's poem seems to be saying that humans control their destiny while Yeats seems to say that humans are controlled by fate. Today I want to show you a strategy for digging a little deeper into what both Frost and Yeats are saying in their poems. The strategy is 'drawing conclusions.' As readers, we know that authors are trying to get us to think in certain ways without actually stating it directly. To get as much meaning as possible, we must actively question what the author is trying to get us to think. The secret to doing this is to think about the topic and what the author is saying and to use our own experience to predict, 'If I were the author and I were saying this about the topic, what would I be thinking, and what would I want my reader to think?' First, I'll use 'The Road Not Taken' to show you how I draw conclusions. Then we'll look at other parts of Frost's poem and at Yeats's poem again as you try to draw your own conclusions with less help from me."

MODELING THE THINKING

Say something like:

"We have already decided that Frost is using the road as a metaphor for life and that the fork in the road was a choice. But being good comprehenders also means being alert for deeper conclusions the author wants us to draw. For instance, consider these lines, upon encountering two alternative ways in the path:

> Oh, I kept the first for another day!
> Yet knowing how way leads on to way,
> I doubted if I should ever come back.

"I know that the poem is about life and that the fork in the path is a choice in life. But what does Frost want me to think when he writes these lines? To build that meaning, I have to look at the words and use my own experience. He says he kept one fork in the road for another day. My experience says that he plans to travel down the other path at some other time. But then he says he doubts that he will ever come back. So, now I have to predict what Frost wants me to conclude here. I know he is talking about life and choices in life. And he says he will do the other road at another time but then says he probably won't be back. To figure out what he is telling me, I think about my own experience. Have I ever said I would do something and really meant to return to do it but then failed to get around to it? If that is my experience, I predict that Frost is saying the same thing about choices in life. He wants me to draw the conclusion that when we choose one thing in life, we seldom get a chance to return to do the thing we set aside. So I predict he wants me to conclude that life is a matter of choices humans make but that, once we make one choice, we can't go back to do something else.

"Do you see how I used the topic and my own experience with what the author said to figure out what conclusions Frost wants me to draw there?"

SCAFFOLDED ASSISTANCE

Example 1: Extensive Teacher Help

Say something like:

"Now, let's look at another example, but this time you help me draw the conclusions. Let's look at the first two lines in the last stanza. Frost says:

I shall be telling this with a sigh
Somewhere ages and ages hence:

"I think Frost wants me to draw a conclusion here. So let's use our strategy for how to draw a conclusion. First, remind yourselves of the topic. Yes, it is life's choices. Then look at the clues he provides. He says he will be telling this (meaning his choice of which road to take) 'with a sigh.' How can I figure out what Frost wants me to conclude here? Yes, we have to think of our own experience. When we do something 'with a sigh,' what do we mean? Okay, for some of you it means that you are sad. Or some of you say it means there are regrets. So if saying it 'with a sigh' means sadness or regrets for you and me, it may also mean that for Frost. But then we have to think what he is sad about, or what he regrets. Are there clues to that? Yes, he is talking about two choices in the poem. He is probably sad or regretful that he couldn't travel both roads, or he may be wondering how things would be different if he had taken the other path."

Example 2: Less Teacher Help

Say something like:

> "Now, let's look at the last two lines of the poem and decide what
> conclusion Frost wants us to draw. What do we need to do first?
> Yes, we know that writers want us to be drawing conclusions as
> we read, so we need to keep the topic in mind and ask ourselves
> what Frost wants us to think at this point. And what will we use
> as clues? Yes, we have to use our own prior knowledge about what
> he says to try to figure out what he wants us to conclude. What
> does he say? Yes, he says it was important to take the road that
> few people traveled. Using your experience, what conclusion do
> you suppose he wants us to draw about ourselves? Yes, it makes
> sense that he is saying that we too should not follow the crowd
> and should make choices that may be different from those that
> other people make."

Example 3: No Teacher Help

Once students are conscious of how to draw conclusions, they can
reread "An Irish Airman Foresees His Death." They can be directed
to draw conclusions at several points in the poem, but they should be
doing the thinking independently of you, and they should be able to
report the reasoning they used to draw the conclusion.

APPLICATION IN READING

This example describes how a literature selection can be read first and
then revisited to learn a strategy. In this particular eighth-grade situation, the application will occur as the teacher and students continue to
study the role fate plays in the lives of human beings. Other literature
selections will be read, and other conclusions will be drawn. As the
class moves later to other units, the teacher will ensure that students
continue to use the strategy of drawing conclusions.

Adapting This Example to Other Situations

This example is situated in an advanced literature class in the middle school where eighth graders are drawing very sophisticated conclusions. But younger students can also learn to draw conclusions using material appropriate to their level. For instance, a kindergarten teacher might share with her children the big book titled *In the Tall, Tall Grass*, by Denise Fleming (Holt, 1991). Following an initial reading, the teacher could return to the text and explain the strategy of drawing conclusions. The process would be basically the same as in the eighth grade, but the language would be appropriate to kindergartners and to the book being used, and the conclusion being drawn would be much less complex. For instance, students will still think about the topic, the clues the author provides, and what those clues make the reader think, and the conclusion will be something like "The author wants us to understand that there are lots of things out there in the grass."

Similarly, readers draw conclusions in expository text. For instance, eighth graders reading the social studies textbook *World Geography and Cultures* (Globe Fearon, 1994) encounter a discussion about using the earth's resources on pages 23 and 24, in which a distinction is made between "renewable" and "nonrenewable" resources. While the text does not state it explicitly, readers can draw conclusions regarding the consequences of using all our "nonrenewable" resources.

HOW WILL YOU KNOW THE LESSON HAS BEEN SUCCESSFUL?

You will know this lesson has been successful when you observe students using their prior knowledge to decide what authors want the reader to think even though it is not explicitly stated in the text, and they can describe how they came to those conclusions.

APPLICATION IN WRITING

In learning to draw conclusions, students are encouraged to "put themselves in the writer's shoes" and to think about what the writer wanted them to conclude. In that sense, the writer (and writing) has already been a part of the drawing conclusion strategy. Students become more adept at drawing conclusions when this connection to writing is emphasized. Engaging students in composing text in which they consciously think about the conclusions they want their readers to draw will help them to be better writers and will strengthen their ability to draw conclusions as readers.

EXAMPLE 14

Evaluating

Good comprehension is not limited to determining an author's message. Comprehension also involves making judgments about the message. The reader evaluates what the author is saying.

Evaluating is a sophisticated thinking strategy, but it can be learned at all grade levels. Kindergarten students, for instance, can begin doing evaluative thinking in listening situations. A typical example is when young children decide whether a story is "fact or fantasy." They make a judgment about whether what happened in the story was real.

In the upper grades, evaluative thinking becomes more complex. Students learn to discern when an author is trying to influence their opinions through use of propaganda or other rhetorical devices, and they learn to go beyond the boundaries of the text, bringing world knowledge to bear on what has been read in order to appraise, critique, or choose alternative conclusions.

Evaluating is particularly important in today's "Information Age." We are constantly bombarded in listening, viewing, and reading situations with information designed to influence us in one way or another. The old saying about "not believing everything you read" (or everything you hear, or everything you view) is more important than ever. Consequently, evaluating is a crucial comprehension strategy.

How Will You Know You Need to Teach Evaluating?

The situation: You note that students accept what they read at face value or justify positions by saying things such as "I believe it because it says so in the book."

The data you collect: Give students short passages and ask them questions requiring them to use their judgment. Sample questions include:

- Do you agree or disagree with the author on that point?
- What do you think they should have done to solve that problem?
- What does the author want you to believe? Do you?

If students are unable to answer questions such as these, they may profit from explanations on how to evaluate what they read.

Explaining the Forest as Well as the Trees

Big understandings you might need to explain when teaching evaluating:

- That not everything you read is factual or true.
- That it is acceptable to disagree with what one reads, and that good readers make judgments about what they read.
- That evaluating requires assertive, proactive thinking.

KEEPING THE MAIN THING THE MAIN THING

This example assumes a fifth-grade setting. The teacher and students are engaged in a unit on the environment. The goal of the study is to decide what action students could take regarding environmental issues. The class has been divided into four reading groups, with each group reading selections matching their reading levels and then sharing the results of their reading in a common effort to decide what action to take. The example that follows focuses on a group that is reading from an anthology titled *Taking a Stand: Integrating Themes in Literature and Language* (Kendall/Hunt, 1993) that includes a section on environmental issues. Today they are going to read an expository selection titled "Acid Rain: The Unsettled Question" (pp. 290–295), have a conversation about the issue of acid rain, and make plans for what they will share with their classmates. Because acid rain is an "unsettled question," the teacher decides to combine the discussion with an explanation of how to make evaluative judgments about what has been read.

The Student's Objective

By the end of this lesson, you will be able to read a selection and take a position regarding acid rain, and you will be able to describe the thinking you do to make your judgments.

What Is the "Secret" to Doing It?

Students must:

- ◆ Read what the text says.
- ◆ Use their own experience background to note if there are gaps or inconsistencies or flaws in the logic.
- ◆ Based on their prior knowledge, answer questions such as "What do I think about this? Do I agree? Do I have a different view?"

LESSON INTRODUCTION

Say something like:

"Our job is to learn about acid rain and report back to the rest of the class about whether there is any action we can take regarding acid rain and the environment. To do so, we are going to read the selection in our anthology about acid rain beginning on page 290. By using prior knowledge about 'acid' and 'rain,' we can make predictions regarding what this article is about. But the title also says that it is 'the unsettled question.' So there must be something that needs to be settled or decided. Let's read this short article silently to find out what needs to be settled. Then we are going to take a position regarding the unsettled question and whether we should take any action about it."

MODELING THE THINKING

After a short discussion of the article's content, say something like:

"We have decided that the unsettled question about acid rain is that in 1988 [when this article was written] the United States and Canada had not worked out an agreement about acid rain. In understanding that, we have the basic message the author wanted us to get. But good readers do not stop there. They go beyond what the author says and make judgments about what they are reading. This is called 'evaluative thinking.' I'll show you how I make these judgments so you will be able to make judgments as you decide what to say to the rest of the class about acid rain.

"We have learned in past lessons that questioning while you read is an important comprehension strategy, especially when we are questioning whether the text makes sense. Evaluative thinking also requires questioning, but the 'secret' now is to ask, 'What do I think about this?' 'Do I agree?' 'Do I have a different view?' I answer these questions by thinking about my own experience and my own preferences and opinions. For instance, when I am reading along on page 292, I find that acid rain damages fish and is suspected of damaging trees and maple syrup. So I'm saying to myself, 'My opinion is that I don't like to hear about fish and trees being damaged. This sounds like a serious problem. We should fix this problem.' So I have already made a judgment. I'm saying to myself as I read that this problem should be fixed. But then I read on to page 293, where it says that Canada proposed to reduce sulfur dioxide emissions if the United States would do the same, but the United States rejected the idea. Now I am questioning again. What do I think about this? What is my opinion? I think about my own views, and at first I say, 'I am upset that the United States rejected Canada's offer. They are not trying to fix the problem.' But then I think more about what it says and what it doesn't say. For instance, it doesn't say *why* the United States rejected the proposal. My experience tells me that there must have been a reason. But the author does not tell me the reason. So I say to myself, 'Why wouldn't the author tell me the reason? In my experience, sometimes people try to influence you by not giving you all the facts. So maybe the author doesn't tell me why because he is trying to get me to think that the United States was wrong to reject the proposal.' I go beyond the information the author provides me to make a judgment of my own.

"Do you see what I'm doing as I think back on the text? I am looking at what the author is saying, I am thinking about gaps or inconsistencies (such as not telling the reason why the United States rejected Canada's proposal), and then I use my experience and my views to make my own evaluative judgment about what the author is saying."

SCAFFOLDED ASSISTANCE

Example 1: Extensive Teacher Help

Say something like:

> "Now let's see if we can make judgments about what you read. Remember that evaluating calls for *your* opinion or *your* judgment. Your opinion or judgment may be different from mine or from the opinion of a friend. But that's okay as long as your thinking makes sense and you can justify the judgment you make. Let's reread the bottom of page 293, where it says that industry did not want to install pollution control devices because they cost a lot of money. Here's a place where we should be evaluating. What must we do first? Yes, we have to examine the statement to see if there are gaps or omissions or inconsistencies. So is there anything there that you question? Anything that is a gap or that is omitted? Okay,

we are not told *how* costly it would be for industry. So, then, you each have to use your experience to decide what you think about this. For instance, some of you may value fish and trees and the environment so much that you think industry should install the devices no matter how expensive they are. Others of you may be thinking that if it is very expensive, industries might go bankrupt, so not paying for the devices might be sensible. There is no right answer. You must examine what the author says and use your own background and your own opinion to evaluate what the author says. So what position did you take? Explain your reasoning to us."

Example 2: Less Teacher Help

Say something like:

"Let's reread another example from this article. But this time you should be evaluating with less help from me. Reread the last paragraph on page 294. What do you think about the last statement that says in 1987 the United States did not agree about a timetable for acid rain reduction. Is this a place where we might want to use our evaluating strategy? What should we do first? Okay, are there gaps or omissions that you might question? Now, what do we think about next? Okay, what does your background or opinion lead you to think here? Can you describe your thinking so that it justifies the judgment you are making?"

Example 3: No Teacher Help

If you observe that students are evaluating what they read and justifying their thinking, you can direct the students to do evaluative thinking with no assistance from you. For instance, they could read the last two paragraphs of the article on page 295 and make judgments about the author's intentions and what action the author would say the class should take regarding acid rain.

APPLICATION IN READING

This example is another illustration of how a text can be read first and a strategy can be applied following the reading of a selection. In this example the group will continue to make evaluative judgments as they discuss what they should recommend to their classmates when they make their report about acid rain. In future units the teacher will continue to ask students to make evaluative judgments as they reflect on what they have read.

Adapting This Example to Other Situations

This example assumed a fifth-grade class reading a short expository text from an anthology. It requires a fairly high level of evaluative thinking because readers must analyze the text for flaws in reasoning and then use their own background and opinions in reaction.

But evaluating is a strategy that can be learned and applied at all grade levels and in narrative as well as expository text. For instance, the big book titled *The Wheels on the Bus*, by Maryann Kovalski (Trumpet Club, 1987), provides several opportunities for young children to apply prior knowledge to evaluate whether story scenes could have really happened the way they are described.

Higher grades, of course, offer even more opportunities for students to evaluate. For instance, middle school teachers could use Gary Larson's *There's a Hair in My Dirt* (HarperCollins, 1998). At a very simple level, encountering worms that sit down to eat a dinner of dirt calls for an evaluative statement about whether this is fact or fantasy. But higher level students can also evaluate the validity of Larson's moral or the appropriateness of the lesson he seems to want to get across.

HOW WILL YOU KNOW THE LESSON
HAS BEEN SUCCESSFUL?

You will know this lesson has been successful if, in reading text in the future, students make evaluative statements about what they have read and justify their statements by describing how they used their background to make a judgment.

APPLICATION IN WRITING

Evaluative thinking is applicable to both writing and reading. Writers often try to convince readers of a particular viewpoint; readers must decide when authors are trying to convince them of something. Students become better evaluators of what they read when they themselves have engaged in composing persuasive text using various rhetorical devices to convince readers of a position.

EXAMPLE 15

Synthesizing

Being literate in the 21st century means being able to combine information within a source or across several different sources. To make sense of it all, it is necessary to synthesize, or combine, information. In this sense, synthesizing is creative. That is, readers must *create* a single understanding from a variety of sources.

Synthesizing is most often used after reading. In the lower grades, synthesizing may combine ideas from *within* a single text. For instance, students could create a new story character embodying traits of the two main story characters. Most often, however, synthesizing involves combining ideas *across* texts. For instance, sixth-grade students might create a composite of life in ancient Egypt after reading three different texts on early Egyptian times, one a short expository article in an anthology, one a textbook chapter, and one a historical fiction.

Synthesizing often results in a product. That is, we usually synthesize because we are creating something new or producing a solution to a problem. For instance, students synthesize when they combine together the information they have learned about botany and use it to plant a garden. Similarly, students synthesize when they use what they have learned about water pollution to create a report that will be delivered to the town board. Consequently, synthesizing is learned best when it is situated within a problem focus in which students are engaged in resolving an issue or in taking action.

How Will You Know You Need to Teach Synthesizing?

The situation: You observe that students cannot compose a statement combining information from two or more sources or that they have difficulty creating a diagram combining information from different sources.

The data you collect: Give students descriptions of two situations; ask them to put them together and state what it is they have in common. Alternatively, give students two recipes for a dish and ask them to create a third that draws on both recipes.

Explaining the Forest as Well as the Trees

Big understandings you might need to explain when teaching synthesizing:

- That different information about a common problem can come from different sources.
- That being a good reader and thinker requires using information from several sources at once.
- That reading is not so much *receiving* understandings as it is *creating* understandings.
- That information can be grouped together, or classified, by common characteristics.

KEEPING THE MAIN THING THE MAIN THING

This example is set in a fourth-grade classroom. For several weeks the teacher and students have been thinking and talking about diversity. The genesis for the discussion was an incident in which some children in the class made fun of certain other children because of perceived differences. The teacher used this as a "teachable moment" for developing tolerance and cultural understanding. Consequently, over the course of a week, she read to the class, and discussed, books such as Janell Cannon's *Stellaluna* (Harcourt Brace, 1993), Bill Martin Jr.'s *I Am Freedom's Child* (Trumpet, 1970), Michelle Maria Surat's

Angel Child, Dragon Child (Scholastic, 1983), Eve Bunting's *Fly Away Home* (Clarion, 1991), and Naomi Shihab Nye's *Sitti's Secrets* (Aladdin, 1994). Because her goal is to extend students' understandings of the individual stories to create a single broad principle about tolerance, and because she knows her students have little experience with combining ideas, she decides to teach a lesson on synthesizing.

The Student's Objective

By the end of this lesson, you will be able to combine ideas from several stories into a single message that fits all the stories, and you will be able to describe the thinking you did to do that.

What Is the "Secret" to Doing It?

Students must:

- ♦ Think about the content of each story.
- ♦ Decide how the stories are alike and different.
- ♦ Identify common elements.
- ♦ Use experience about the common elements to create a synthesis.

LESSON INTRODUCTION

Say something like:

> "We have been reading and talking about five stories about animals and children that were different from other animals or children. Today we are going to look across all five stories and decide how they can be combined together to make one broad statement that is true of all the stories. This is called 'synthesizing.' It is an important comprehension strategy because good readers and good thinkers often need to combine ideas from different places in

order to decide what is important. We are trying to combine ideas from five different stories to decide how to respond to people who are different. I am going to show you a strategy for synthesizing using two of the books we have read. Then I am going to have you try the strategy yourselves using the other three books we have read. The secret to doing this is that you must think about what is the same about the stories and then use your own experience to decide whether there is a common message across the two stories."

MODELING THE THINKING

Say something like:

"Let's start with these two books: *Stellaluna* and *Angel Child, Dragon Child*. I want to synthesize the ideas in these two books. That means I want to put the two books together to see if there is a single idea that fits them both. To do that, I first think about what was different about the two stories. *Stellaluna* was about a bat and some birds; *Angel Child, Dragon Child* was about a Vietnamese girl in her first American school. So they are different in that way. And what happens to Stellaluna is not what happens to Ut. But then I think about what is alike in the two stories. *Stellaluna* was about a bat who had to live with birds but ends up being friends with them; *Angel Child, Dragon Child* was about a Vietnamese girl who had to go to school with Americans but ends up being friends with Raymond. Stellaluna felt different among the birds; Ut felt different among the Americans. But they both made friends. So now I must use my own knowledge about friends to decide what message fits both stories. I know that friends like each other. So the common message here must be that people who are different can still like each other."

SCAFFOLDED ASSISTANCE

Example 1: Extensive Teacher Assistance

Say something like:

> "Now let's see if you can synthesize by combining a third story with the two I just did. This time you help me. Let's think together about *Fly Away Home*. Is this story different than *Stellaluna* and *Angel Child, Dragon Child*? Yes, *Fly Away Home* is about a boy and his father who live in the airport because they don't have a home. That's really different from bats, and it's really different from a Vietnamese girl going to an American school! But let's think about how *Fly Away Home* is similar. Andrew in *Fly Away Home* lives in an airport. Is living in an airport normal? No, that is really different. Stellaluna was different because she was a bat among birds, and Ut was different because she was a Vietnamese among Americans. And Andrew is different because he lives in an airport. But we liked Stellaluna and Ut and Andrew even though they were different. So, if you use your own knowledge, can you decide what message is the same across all three stories? Yes, maybe it is that we can like someone despite the differences."

Example 2: Less Teacher Help

Say something like:

> "Let's try another one, but this time you must do more of the thinking and I will provide less help. Let's try to synthesize *Sitti's Secrets* with the three books we have already discussed. When we think about *Sitti's Secrets*, we know it is different from the other stories. But how is *Sitti's Secrets* like those other stories? Is this also a story about someone who is different? Yes, it is. So use your own feelings and knowledge about Sitti. How do you feel about her? Is this similar to how you feel about Stellaluna and Ut and Andrew? So what must the common message be across all four of these stories?"

Example 3: No Teacher Help

Once students begin demonstrating the ability to synthesize, have them try it on their own. For instance, have them consider *I Am Freedom's Child* and whether the message is the same as the message in the other stories discussed. Then have them describe the thinking they did to make their decision.

APPLICATION IN READING

In this example students learn and apply synthesizing following the reading of the stories. However, the teacher will ensure that students continue to apply the synthesizing strategy in other situations.

Adapting This Example to Other Situations

Synthesizing can be done in a legitimate form at all grade levels and using sources other than narrative text. For instance, first graders studying plants could read an expository text such as *Plants and Seeds*, by Colin Walker (Wright Group, 1992), and view a video on planting gardens. Then they could combine the two together into a list of things they must remember to do when planting their classroom garden. Similarly, seventh graders studying state government could synthesize information obtained from their social studies textbook and from a visit by the local representative to the state legislature. In all situations the "secret" continues to be looking for similarities and using prior knowledge to combine the information into a single coherent message.

HOW WILL YOU KNOW THE LESSON
HAS BEEN SUCCESSFUL?

You will know the lesson has been successful if, in future situations involving the combining of information from several sources, students are able to create a common message and can describe the thinking they did to accomplish it.

APPLICATION IN WRITING

Synthesizing is just as important in writing situations as in reading situations. Writing reports of social studies topics, for instance, requires combining together information gathered from a variety of sources. Similarly, writing a narrative often involves integrating into a single story various kinds of information. The more experience students have integrating multiple sources into their writing, the better they will be at synthesizing information they read, or hear, or view.

Examples for Explaining Word Recognition

Attending to Print Detail

Reading is, among other things, a visual task. Readers must look at the squiggles on the page and see how they are different. Some children have little experience with distinguishing one squiggle from another. Students who lack the ability to visually discriminate among like forms—that is, they do not attend to the print detail that distinguishes one letter squiggle from another—may need explicit help.

This is a skill of knowing how to look. For instance, some young students look at letters such as *b*, *d*, and *p* and do not "see" how they are different. They do not look different to them because they do not know how to look.

The key in attending to print detail is to look for differences, not similarities. It is the differences that set one form or letter squiggle apart from another. Consequently, when students require assistance in attending to print detail, the explanation focuses on helping them note differences.

How Will You Know You Need to Teach Print Detail?

The situation: Students will say one letter for another (e.g., will mix up the letters *d* and *b*) or will reverse letters or otherwise write them incorrectly in their writing.

The data you collect: Note students' writing of letter forms and whether they say the correct name for letters.

Explaining the Forest as Well as the Trees

Big understandings you might need to explain when teaching print detail:

♦ The concepts of "same" and "different."

♦ That letters are like code, and in order for the code to be read correctly, the letters always have to be made the same way.

KEEPING THE MAIN THING THE MAIN THING

This example is set in a kindergarten class. The children's project for the day is to learn to follow simple directions when making mudpies. In preparation for doing so, the teacher shares the big book *How to Make a Mudpie*, by Rozanne Lanczak Williams and Keith Berger (Creative Teaching Press, 1995). But because the teacher has collected assessment data indicating that these students do not always attend to fine differences in print, she also decides to use this text as an opportunity to develop letter discrimination.

The Student's Objective

By the end of this lesson, you will be able to tell an *m* from an *n* and you will be able to say how they are different.

What Is the "Secret" to Doing It?

Students must:

♦ Note the visual differences that distinguish one form from another.

LESSON INTRODUCTION

Say something like:

"We have already talked about the fact that we are going to make mudpies today, and in order to do that we must follow some directions. We are going to read this big book together because it describes the steps we must follow to make mudpies. But before we start reading this book, I want to show you how to look closely at letters so you can tell one from another. Being able to do that is very important for being able to read books like this big book on mudpies. What I'm going to show you today is how to tell an *m* from an *n* because there are both *m*'s and *n*'s in the book we are going to read today. The secret is to look at how they are different. Watch and I'll show you how to do this."

MODELING THE THINKING

Say something like:

"Pay close attention to what I do because I will be asking you to tell *m*'s from *n*'s when we read our book about mudpies. I am writing an *m* and an *n* on the board. In order to tell these letters apart, we must use our eyes and look for differences between them. When I look at the letter *m*, I see two humps. I'm going to put a little ✕ over each hump so I remember how many there are. When I look at the letter *n*, I see only one hump. So I put a little ✕ over that one hump. The *m* and the *n* look very much alike because they both have humps. But they are not exactly the same. The *m* has two humps, but the *n* has only one hump. So I can tell them apart because they have a different number of humps."

SCAFFOLDED ASSISTANCE

Example 1: Extensive Teacher Help

Say something like:

> "Let's see if you can tell *m*'s from *n*'s and tell me why they are different. I will give you lots of help this time by leaving my little ×'s on the humps. When I point to a letter, tell me whether it is an *m* or an *n* and count the number of humps so you can tell me how you know they are different."

Example 2: Less Teacher Help

Say something like:

> "Now I'm going to make it harder. Let's see if you can tell which is an *m* and which is an *n* if I remove the little ×'s. Now when I point to a letter, you must tell me which it is and how you know, but you don't have the little ×'s to help you count the humps."

Example 3: No Teacher Help

Once students have demonstrated the ability to distinguish one letter form from the other, have them identify *m*'s and *n*'s in *How to Make a Mudpie.* Read the book to them first for information about how to make mudpies, but then return to the text to have them identify *m*'s and *n*'s.

APPLICATION IN READING

This example illustrates how a skill can be taught before applying it in a book. The skill of discriminating one letter from another is applied to the book on mudpies today. However, the teacher will also look for other opportunities on subsequent days to apply what has been learned when reading other texts.

Adapting This Example to Other Situations

This skill is emphasized at the very early stages of reading acquisition. However, it is also occasionally important to revisit this skill at later stages. For instance, second-, third-, and fourth-grade students who repeatedly mix up look-alike words such as *though* and *through* often do so because they are not attending to the print detail and noting the presence or absence of the letter *r* as the third letter in the word.

HOW WILL YOU KNOW THE LESSON HAS BEEN SUCCESSFUL?

You will know the lesson has been successful when you note that students no longer mix up letters when identifying them and/or no longer reverse letters or otherwise form them incorrectly in their writing, and when they can describe how they knew one letter form was different from the other.

APPLICATION IN WRITING

The more students write letters and practice doing so correctly, the faster and more accurately they will discriminate one letter form from another in print. Consequently, the more often we engage students in writing letter forms, the better they will be at "reading" them.

EXAMPLE 17

Recognizing Words at Sight

All good readers instantly recognize and name most of the words they encounter in print. That is, they recognize words "at sight."

The ability to recognize words instantly is important from the earliest stages of reading. Emergent readers, for instance, must instantly recognize such common words as *the, come, have, do,* and *here,* none of which can be figured out by using phonic rules. In a time when much emphasis is placed on phonics, it is important to remember that the primary way to recognize words is by knowing them at sight. For instance, the generally accepted standard for placing students in reading material for instructional purposes is their ability to recognize at sight 90–95% of the words on the page. Hence, remembering sight words is a crucial reading skill.

The first goal in sight word instruction is to help students remember the 300 or so most common words in the language. This is emphasized during the early stages of reading acquisition. But in the long run the goal is to develop an understanding that good readers ultimately remember almost all the words they are likely to encounter in routine, daily reading. Good instruction in sight word recognition therefore not only results in the acquisition of a stock of words that are recognized instantly, but also develops the concept that most words should ultimately become sight words.

The best way to learn to recognize words at sight is to do lots and lots of easy reading that employs the words to be learned. During the early stages, repeatedly reading favorite books is a helpful technique because, in the process of doing so, students learn to recognize words instantly.

However, some children need more than abundant easy reading in order to remember sight words. For those children, it is sometimes necessary to provide an explanation and much repetition in seeing and saying the words. This example is an illustration of such instruction.

How Will You Know You Need to Teach Sight Words?

The situation: Students will pause for extended periods when encountering common words, or will try to sound the words out, or will request the teacher to tell them what the words are. They will not say the words instantly.

The data you collect: When listening to students read orally, note the specific words students do not recognize instantly. If they are common words, they should be learned as sight words.

Explaining the Forest as Well as the Trees

Big understandings you might need to explain when teaching sight words:

- ♦ That good readers recognize most words instantly.
- ♦ That sight word recognition is a task of "looking and saying," not a task of sounding out a word.
- ♦ That the ultimate goal in word recognition is to know as many words as possible at sight.

KEEPING THE MAIN THING THE MAIN THING

This example assumes a first-grade setting. The class is doing a project on different kinds of animals so they can produce a book for the classroom library titled *How Different Animals Are Different*. They will dictate the text to the teacher and will do the illustrations themselves. In pursuit of this topic, they are reading *Legs, Legs, Legs*, by Carol

Krueger (Lands End Publishing, 1993), a book that distinguishes among various animals by the number of legs they have. Because the word *legs* will be used often in this project, the teacher wants students to recognize the word at sight.

The Student's Objective

By the end of this lesson, you will be able to recognize and say the new word *legs* instantly every time you see it in the animal book we are going to be reading today, and you will be able to say how you remembered it.

What Is the "Secret" to Doing It?

Students must:

♦ Note the visual form of the word, especially its beginning and ending.
♦ Repeatedly look at the word and say it.

LESSON INTRODUCTION

Say something like:

"As we have been reading about animals in order to write our own book for the classroom library, we have been learning lots of new words. We have also been learning that good readers remember these words and say them instantly whenever they see them in a book or other writing. Today we are going to read a book together. This book will give us lots of important information about how different animals are different, so we will be able to use what we learn when we write our own books. But this book also uses a new word we will be using often. So before we start reading the book let's learn this new word. Remember that the 'secret' is to pay close attention to what the word looks like, especially at the beginning and the end. We want to remember this word so you will be able to say it as soon as you see it in the book we will read today."

MODELING THE THINKING

Say something like:

> "The new word we are going to learn is *legs*. I am writing it here on the board. Let me show you how I remember words like this. I have to remember what it looks like, so I look closely at the letters in the word. The 'secret' is to look especially hard at the beginning and the ending of the word. When I look at the beginning, I see the letter *l*. I close my eyes and picture the beginning letter in my mind. Then I look at the ending. I see the letters *g* and *s* at the end. So I close my eyes again and picture the ending letters in my mind. Then, with my eyes closed, I use my finger to write out on the rug in front of me the word I see in my mind, saying the word as I write it. Then I look at the word on the board and see if what I wrote looks the same as the word on the board."

SCAFFOLDED ASSISTANCE

Example 1: Extensive Teacher Help

Say something like:

> "Let's see if you can do as I did. Look carefully at the word as I have written it on the board. Now close your eyes. What do you see as the first letter in the word? Okay. Now look at the word again, and then close your eyes. What do you see as the last letters in the word? Good. Now use your finger to trace the letters in the word on the rug in front of you, and say the word out loud as you write it."

Example 2: Less Teacher Help

Say something like:

"I have two index cards here. On one I have printed the word *legs* in the correct way. On the other, I have used the same letters but I have mixed them up. It doesn't say *legs* because the letters are not in the right order. I'm going to show each card to you for just a second or two. I won't show it to you for longer than a second or two because what we are learning is to recognize the word *legs* instantly. If the card I show is the word *legs*, say 'legs.' If the card I show does not have the letters in the right order, don't say anything. We'll do this several times to give you practice looking at and saying the word when it is written correctly."

Example 3: No Teacher Help

Once students are recognizing the word correctly, begin reading the book *Legs, Legs, Legs*. Give each student an opportunity to point to and say the word *legs* when it appears in the text, or, alternatively, have the students read the book in unison with you. Your goal is to give each student multiple opportunities to encounter the word *legs* in text and to say it correctly without hesitation.

APPLICATION IN READING

This example demonstrates how a skill can be developed prior to reading a text. After students apply the new sight word in reading the text for that day, the teacher will want to ensure that students continue to encounter the word in text they read on subsequent days.

Adapting This Example to Other Situations

This example is set in a first-grade class and assumes that the students need very explicit help on how to remember words. In higher grades and/or with different students, sight words may be developed with less specificity. For instance, third graders reading Mem Fox's *Possum Magic* (The Trumpet Club, 1983) may not know *invisible* as a sight word or may mix up the word *through* with the look-alike word *though*. But because they are more experienced in learning to remember words, it may only be necessary to point out the visual features of the words and provide a minimum of repetitions.

HOW WILL YOU KNOW THE LESSON
HAS BEEN SUCCESSFUL?

You will know that students have learned to recognize specific words as sight words if, during their reading of real text, they say the word quickly and without hesitation. If the students are reading silently, you may time their reading. If they take a long time to read a particular selection, they may be struggling over words that should be remembered at sight.

APPLICATION IN WRITING

One of the best ways for children to learn to recognize words instantly is to ensure that they use the words in their writing. Anything a teacher can do to have students use new words in their writing will enhance the instant recognition of these words whenever they are encountered in reading.

Phonemic Awareness

Phonemic awareness is the ability to distinguish among sounds. It is a crucial prerequisite to phonics because you cannot use letter sounds to figure out an unknown word if you cannot tell one sound from another. It is totally an auditory skill. The goal is that students will hear the differences in sounds. Consequently, students use only their ears, not their eyes.

Phonemic awareness is a prereading skill and is most often taught to emergent readers. However, some children come to school already knowing how to discriminate among sounds because they have played sound games at home, have sung rhyming songs, have had stories read to them containing funny sounds, and have engaged in other activities involving discrimination among sounds.

Children who have not had such experience prior to school, however, will need to develop phonemic awareness skills. This involves being able to match rhyming words, being able to tell when words end or begin with the same sound, being able to segment words into separate sounds, and being able to blend sounds together.

The following example illustrates how one might explain one type of phonemic awareness, that of discriminating among like and different sounds at the beginning of words.

How Will You Know You Need to Teach Phonemic Awareness?

The situation: Students cannot tell whether words you say sound the same or different at the beginning.

The data you collect: Say two words and ask students to tell you whether they are the same or different at the beginning and to say the sound (not the letter name) they hear at the beginning.

Explaining the Forest as Well as the Trees

Big understandings you might need to explain when teaching phonemic awareness:

♦ What it means to "rhyme."
♦ The concepts of "beginning" and "end."
♦ The concepts of "same" and "different."

KEEPING THE MAIN THING THE MAIN THING

This example is set in a kindergarten class. During "show and tell," one of the students reported that he saw pictures of whales migrating on television the night before. This resulted in a lively discussion on whales. The teacher had already collected data indicating that this group of children needed help determining whether words began with the same sound or different sounds. She decides to use the discussion of whales as a "teachable moment" for developing this phonemic awareness skill. She uses her *Big Book Magazine* on whales (Issue Number 1, Scholastic, 1989).

Remember, letters and letter names are not part of this lesson. Phonemic awareness is sound-only.

The Student's Objective

By the end of this lesson, you will be able to tell whether a word I say begins with the same sound or a different sound, and say the sound you hear at the beginning.

What Is the "Secret" to Doing It?

Students must:

♦ Separate the beginning sound from the ending of the word.

♦ Emphasize the beginning sound.

LESSON INTRODUCTION

Say something like:

"All our talk about whales reminds me of one of my favorite poems. It is on the front page of this *Big Book Magazine* about whales. Listen while I read this poem to you, and try to figure out what the author of the poem is saying about the whale's tail. After we discuss the poem, we will listen to some of the words the poet uses and decide whether they sound the same or different at the beginning."

MODELING THE THINKING

Say something like:

"Now that we've finished discussing this poem about whales, I want to show you how to tell whether words sound the same or different at the beginning. This is an important skill to learn if you are going to be able to read books like this yourselves. Listen carefully to what I do so you too can listen to words and tell whether they sound the same or different at the beginning.

"In order to tell whether a word is the same or different at the beginning, we must say the word slowly and separate the beginning sound from the rest of the word. For instance, in our poem about a whale, we had the words *whale* and *snail*. They sound very much alike. But I'll say each word slowly: *whhhhh—ale* ... *snnnn—ail*. By stretching the word out and separating out the beginning sound, I can tell that *whale* begins with a *whhhh* sound and that *snail* begins with a *snnnn* sound. So I know they are different because one begins with *whhhh* and the other begins with *snnnn*."

SCAFFOLDED ASSISTANCE

Example 1: Extensive Teacher Help

Say something like:

"Here are two other words from the poem. One is *tail* and the other is the word we used before—*whale*. I'm going to help you this time by separating the beginning sound in the words for you. You listen and tell me if the words are the same or different at the beginning: *T-t-t-ail*.... *Whhhh—ale*. What sound do you hear at the beginning of *t-t-t-ail*? Yes, the sound is *t-t-t*-at the beginning. What sound do you hear at the beginning of *whhhh—ale*. Yes, the sound is *whhhh* at the beginning. So do these words sound the same or different at the beginning? How do you know?"

Example 2: Less Teacher Help

Say something like:

"Now let's try it with two other words that were in the poem: *that* and *there*. This time I'm not going to help you by stretching out the sounds for you. You will have to separate the beginning sound from the ending yourself. Let's see you try it with the word *that*. Now stretch out the word *there*. What sound did you hear at the beginning of *that*? What sound did you hear at the beginning of *there*? Is that the same sound or a different sound?"

Example 3: No Teacher Help

Say something like:

> "Now let's try listening to words in a story in my *Big Book Magazine* on whales. This is the story of Humphrey, the Wrong Way Whale. I'm going to read the story, then we will go back and listen to some of the words in the story, such as *wrong* and *way* and *whale*, to decide whether they begin with the same sound or with different sounds."

APPLICATION IN READING

In this example the skill is taught after reading a poem on whales and is applied again when listening to the story of Humphrey. Ultimately the ability to discriminate among sounds will be applied in the learning of phonics (in tasks such as those illustrated in Example 18). In the meantime, however, teachers should give students opportunities to discriminate among sounds in stories the teacher shares with students on subsequent occasions. Some students will need multiple opportunities to discriminate among sounds.

Adapting This Example to Other Situations

Phonemic awareness is most frequently taught in kindergarten and first grade. However, older students who are just learning how to read, as well as students for whom English is a new language, may also require the same kind of explanation in order to learn to hear the differences in sounds. On rare occasions, older students who have persistent difficulties with phonics may be hampered by an inability to tell the differences in sounds. Such students should also review instruction in phonemic awareness.

HOW WILL YOU KNOW THE LESSON
HAS BEEN SUCCESSFUL?

Students will be able to say whether two words sound the same or different at the beginning, and they will be able to isolate the sound they hear at the beginning of the words and say that sound. Remember, it is the *sound*, not the letter name, that you want them to identify.

APPLICATION IN WRITING

Students who need phonemic awareness are typically writing only squiggle marks on the page or beginning forms of invented spelling. Normally they are not yet writing lots of real words. Nonetheless, the squiggles students write are words to them, and they often happily read those words aloud upon request. On those occasions, students can be asked whether certain pairs of words they use in their writing begin with the same sound or different sounds.

Letter–Sound Association

Phonics instruction begins with learning to tie particular consonant letters to the sounds they typically make. Unlike phonemic awareness, which requires students to pay attention to sound only, learning a letter sound requires students to attend to both the visual form of the letter and the sound it makes.

It is generally best to begin teaching letter sounds after students have demonstrated phonemic awareness (see Example 18) and have learned some common sight words (see Example 17). Using known sight words helps students see how letter sounds are part of real reading. For instance, if kids recognize in print the words *Bill* and *Bob* as the names of fellow students, those known words can be used to help students learn the sound at the beginning of an unknown word such as *Barbara*. While it is possible to teach letter–sound association in isolation from real words and real text, students make better sense of how to use letter sounds if real words and real text are used.

How Will You Know You Need to Teach Letter–Sound Association?

The situation: When students encounter a new word having the particular consonant letter in the initial position, they do not attempt to say the first sound, or they say the sound incorrectly.

The data you collect: Point to a word in a text and ask students to say the first sound in the word.

Explaining the Forest as Well as the Trees

Big understandings you might need to explain when teaching let-ter–sound associations:

- ◆ That different letters have different sounds.
- ◆ That printed text is talk written down.
- ◆ The concept of "code," and that alphabet letters are a code for writing messages.

KEEPING THE MAIN THING THE MAIN THING

This example assumes a first-grade class involved in making their own books about animals. They will read their books orally to "buddies" in the kindergarten. During the project, the teacher supports students' writing efforts by reading various animal stories to the class. One is the big book *Who Is the Beast?*, by Keith Baker (Harcourt Brace Javanovich, 1990). But the teacher also wants to teach students the letter sound /s/. Since *Who Is the Beast?* includes several words that begin with /s/, the teacher decides to use this book as a vehicle for teaching the sound of /s/.

The Student's Objective

By the end of this lesson, you will be able to say the sound of /s/ when you find that letter at the beginning of a word you do not know at sight.

What Is the "Secret" to Doing It?

Students must:

- ◆ Look at the letter while saying the letter sound.

LESSON INTRODUCTION

Say something like:

> "As part of our writing project on animals, I am going to read this big book to you. The title is *Who Is the Beast?* It's a wonderful story with an interesting message. It may give you some ideas you can use when you are writing your own stories. But before we begin, I want to teach you a new letter sound because there are several new words in this story that begin with this letter sound. I'm going to teach you the sound the letter *s* makes at the beginning of most words. The secret to learning letter sounds is to look at the letter as you say the sound."

MODELING THE THINKING

Say something like:

> "We already know some words that begin with the letter *s*. For instance, we know the word *see* and we know the word *say*. Both begin with the sound of /s/. Pay attention to how I learn this letter sound. First, I look at the *s* words I already know. I stretch out the first sound of those words so I can clearly hear what the first letter says. *S-s-s-see* ... *S-s-s-say*. The letter *s* is saying the *s-s-s-s* sound in both these words. So, to remember the sound the /s/ makes, I put my finger on the letter *s*, look at the letter, and say the /s/ sound. *S-s-s-see* ... *S-s-s-say*. To remember the letter sound, I look at the letter at the same time I say the sound."

SCAFFOLDED ASSISTANCE

Example 1: Extensive Teacher Help

Say something like:

> "Here's a new word that begins with /s/ (*point to the word* sound). It is one of the /s/ words we will find in our story today. Let's work together on this one so I can help you. Look at the letter *s*

and together with me say the *s-s-s-s-s*-sound. Ready, look and say *s-s-s-s*. The whole word is *sound*, as in 'I heard a sound.' Let's say the whole word together. First, look at the *s*, say the *s-s-s-s* sound, then say the rest of the word."

Example 2: Less Teacher Help

Say something like:

"Okay, this time I'm not going to give you so much help. You have to do it yourself instead of doing it in unison with me. Here's another /s/ word in the story we are going to read (*point to the word* sight). First, point to the letter *s*. Good. Now, while you are pointing at the letter, say the sound that *s* makes. Good. It makes the *s-s-s-s* sound. The rest of the word says '-ight,' so if we put the *s-s-s-s* sound in front of *-ight*, what does it say? Good. It says 'sight.'"

Example 3: No Teacher Help

Say something like:

"Here are two more /s/ words that appear in our story of *Who Is the Beast?* (*Write on the board the words* so *and* side.) Look at these words and say the sound the first letter makes."

Caution: The word *sure* also appears in the story, but we would not use it because it makes the *sh-sh-sh* sound, not the *s-s-s-s* sound. Similarly, we would not use the word *swing* that appears in the story because it begins with the /sw/ blend, not the /s/ sound.

APPLICATION IN READING

In this example, a teacher teaches the skill first and has students use it when reading a story. When the teacher reads the story, she points out the /s/ words and has students point to the letter and say the *s-s-s-s* sound. Some students will need additional repetitions when the teacher is reading other books on subsequent days.

Adapting This Lesson to Other Situations

Letter–sound association is usually taught in the primary grades. However, some older students may also need to learn certain letter sounds, especially the more difficult sounds such as the two sounds the /th/ digraph makes in words such as *think* and *those,* or the sound of blends such as /str/. If explanation of more difficult letter–sound associations is necessary, the above example can be adapted and used.

How Will You Know the Lesson Has Been Successful?

Students will look at new words beginning with the letter sound and say the correct sound for that letter.

APPLICATION IN WRITING

Letter–sound association is taught in this example as a reading skill. However, letter–sound association is equally applicable to spelling. That is, once a student learns the sound *s* makes, it can be applied not only when encountering a new word in print but also when trying to spell a word that begins with the sound /s/. In this particular example, students would apply what they have learned about the sound of the letter *s* when trying to spell words that begin with the /s/ sound when they write their animal stories.

Decoding by Analogy

Decoding by analogy is a strategy for figuring out words by chunks rather than letter by letter. For instance, a student who knows *each* as a sight word can figure out the unknown word *peach* if he or she knows the consonant sound /p/. The reader first finds the spelling pattern in the unknown word, recognizes it as the known spelling pattern "each," adds the beginning /p/ sound to the pattern, and says the new word. This is called "decoding by analogy" because the new word is figured out by comparing it to a known word. It is also sometimes called an "onset rime," with the *onset* being the beginning consonant and the *rime* being the spelling pattern. It is a strategy because, unlike a skill, it is not done the same way each time. Rather, decoding by analogy requires trial-and-error reasoning by the reader.

While it is possible to sound out words letter by letter rather than by chunking, doing so is a laborious process. Few students become proficient at it because of the numerous variations in vowel sounds. Decoding by analogy minimizes the vowel problem because the known spelling pattern, or rime, includes the vowel sound.

We start teaching decoding by analogy with one-syllable words in the primary grades. At higher reading levels, readers learn to use decoding by analogy as a strategy for figuring out multisyllable words. The following is an example of the former.

How Will You Know You Need to Teach Decoding by Analogy?

The situation: Students are reading text and are unable to figure out unknown one-syllable words that contain common spelling patterns.

The data you collect: Students say the beginning sounds of unknown words but struggle to figure out the rest of the word. They may say the initial consonant sound and guess at the rest of it, or say the initial consonant sound and try to blend together the individual letter sounds. But they are unsuccessful in figuring out the unknown word.

Explaining the Forest as Well as the Trees

Big understandings you might want to explain when teaching decoding by analogy:

- ♦ That decoding by analogy is for "emergency use" when encountering a word that is not a sight word, and that it is not used routinely.
- ♦ That decoding by analogy is preferred to letter-by-letter sounding because it is faster and more accurate.
- ♦ That words sometimes contain familiar spelling patterns, or rimes.

KEEPING THE MAIN THING THE MAIN THING

The example assumes a group of learning-disabled second-grade students who are going to be reading Shel Silverstein's poem "The Dragon of Grindly Grun" from his book *A Light in the Attic* (Harper & Row, 1981). The teacher has previously noted that the students use initial consonant sounds but have difficulty figuring out the rest of the word. The teacher can use this poem to teach decoding by analogy because it has unknown words such as *Grun* and *sun* and *bun* that students can figure out by using the previously learned sight word *run*.

The Student's Objective

By the end of this lesson, you will be able to figure out unknown words in the poem we are going to read by using the spelling patterns of words we know at sight, and you will be able to tell how you figured those words out.

What Is the "Secret" to Doing It?

Students must:

♦ Identify the spelling pattern in the unknown word as one they know from a previously learned sight word.

♦ Insert the beginning sound of the unknown word into the known spelling pattern and then say the new word.

LESSON INTRODUCTION

Say something like:

"We're going to read a funny poem by Shel Silverstein today. But it has some hard words in it that you do not know so I am going to first teach you how to figure out those hard words. The secret to figuring out these words is to see if the unknown word has a familiar spelling pattern or rime at the end and to combine the beginning sound with the rime."

MODELING THE THINKING

Say something like:

"Before we start reading, let me show you how I do it. Let's say I'm reading along and I run into the word *fun*. I don't know that word. So I stop and try to figure it out. I know the sound of the letter *f* so I can make the beginning sound. But I don't know how to say the rest of the word. So I look at the letters in the rest of the word—the *-un*. I say to myself, 'Do I know a sight word that ends in the letters *-un*? Yes, I know the sight word *run*.' So if I take off the *r* in *run*, put *f* in its place, say the sound of /f/and /un/, I end up with the word *fun*. So what you do to figure out unknown words is to look for a rime or spelling pattern in the word that is the same as the spelling pattern in a sight word you know and then take off the first letter, put on the first letter of the new word, and say the rest of the word."

SCAFFOLDED ASSISTANCE

Example 1: Extensive Teacher Help

Say something like:

"I'm going to show you some words that are like the new words we will be seeing in the Shel Silverstein poem we read today. For each of these new words, I have underlined the spelling pattern that is the same as *run* to help you to separate the beginning sound from the rime. What I want you to do is to figure out how to say these words and to tell me how you figured it out. The first word is *spun*."

Example 2: Less Teacher Help

Say something like:

"Here are some more words that are like the new words we will see in the poem we read today. But I am making it harder this time because I have not underlined the spelling pattern. You have to figure out the spelling pattern yourself and think about how you are going to figure out the word. Then you have to tell me how you figured it out. The first word is *stun*."

Example 3: No Teacher Help

Say something like:

"I have written out on cards some sentences. Each of these sentences has a new word in it that uses the spelling pattern we are working on. What you need to do is read the sentence and, when you come to the new word, figure it out using our new strategy. Then I want you to explain to me how you figured it out."

APPLICATION IN READING

This example demonstrates how a strategy can be taught first and then applied to a text. Once students are able to use the spelling pattern to figure out unknown words in a scaffolded situation and can describe the thinking process they are using to successfully figure out the word, they read the Silverstein poem. The teacher also ensures that students use this strategy in subsequent readings of real text.

Adapting This Example to Other Situations

This example assumes a group of learning-disabled second graders. However, other second graders, as well as upper-grade and middle school students who have difficulty sounding out new words, may also profit from explanations about how to decode by analogy.

This example can also be adapted to teach older students how to figure out multisyllable words. Again, the "secret" continues to be examining the word for known spelling patterns or rimes. If the unknown word is *envelope*, the reader can use the known rime *en* to pronounce the first syllable, the known sound of the consonant *v* and the rime *el* to sound out *vel* and the known consonant *l* and the rime -*ope* to sound out *lope*.

HOW WILL YOU KNOW THE LESSON
WAS SUCCESSFUL?

When students encounter unknown words having the same spelling pattern as a word they know at sight, they will figure the word out. When you ask them how they figured it out, they will report that they thought of the known sight word, used the spelling pattern, added in the initial consonant sound, and said the word.

APPLICATION IN WRITING

Decoding by analogy is applicable to spelling as well as to reading. As soon as students can use this strategy to figure out unknown words in a reading situation, they can use it to figure out words they need to spell in their writing. The process is the same. They use a known sight word that has the same sound as the word they are trying to spell, use the ending of the known word to spell the new word, and add in the appropriate beginning consonant.

Frequently Appearing Spelling Patterns					
-ab	-ea	-ice	-oad	-op	-ub
-ack	-eak	-id	-oak	-ope	-uck
-ad	-eal	-ide	-oat	-ound	-ug
-ade	-ean	-ie	-ob	-out	-um
-age	-ear	-ig	-ock	-ow	-un
-ail	-eat	-ight	-od	-own	-ure
-ain	-ed	-ike	-og	-oy	-us
-ait	-ee	-ill	-oice		-ut
-ake	-eed	-im	-oil		
-all	-eel	-ime	-oin		
-ale	-een	-in	-oke		
-am	-eep	-ine	-old		
-ame	-eet	-ing	-ole		
-an	-ell	-ink	-oll		
-and	-en	-tion	-one		
-ap	-end	-ip	-ong		
-at	-ent	-ish	-ook		
-ate	-et	-it	-ool		
-aw	-ite	-oom			

Context and Phonics in Combination

Good readers combine skills and strategies when reading. One common example is the way good readers use context in combination with initial consonant sounds to figure out unknown words in text. When encountering an unknown word, they think about both the sound at the beginning of the unknown word and what would make sense in that context. It is very useful because it can be used quickly, and it frequently results in accurate word identification.

Using context in combination with phonics is a strategy. The reader predicts what the unknown word is by using both prior knowledge about consonant sounds and what is being talked about in the text.

While an important strategy in its own right, context and phonics in combination is also important because it can be used to illustrate how good readers are flexible and fluid in their use of skills and strategies. That is, strategy use is not rule-driven. Being strategic often means combining and predicting in new ways rather than using strategies as if they were rules to be followed. The following example illustrates how this kind of thinking can be started even before children are reading independently.

How Will You Know You Need to Teach Context and Phonics in Combination?

The situation: When a word is encountered in text that begins with a known consonant and is surrounded by context clues, students are not able to figure out the word, or they do so using only the consonant sound or the context rather than both.

The data you collect: Ask students to describe how they figured out unknown words when they were encountered in text, or give them sample sentences in which unknown words begin with a known consonant and are surrounded by strong context clues and ask them to describe how they would figure out what each unknown word is.

Explaining the Forest as Well as the Trees

Big understandings you might need to explain when teaching context and phonics:

- ♦ That good readers stop and solve problems they encounter during the reading of text.
- ♦ That good readers often combine skills and strategies together.

KEEPING THE MAIN THING THE MAIN THING

This lesson occurs as part of a math lesson in the first grade. The class is engaged in a math unit on measurement, and students are measuring various things in the classroom environment. Today they are learning to measure thickness. To develop a concept for thickness, the teacher reads aloud the big book titled *How Big Is Big*, by Avelyn Davidson (Wright Group, 1990), which has a section on thickness (pp. 10 and 11). The teacher also wants to use this book as a place to apply understandings about figuring out unknown words using context and phonics in combination, so before reading the big book she explains how to use context and phonics in combination.

The Student's Objective

By the end of this lesson, you will be able to figure out words you don't know when we are reading about thick things by using what you know about letter sounds and about context, and you will be able to say how you figured out the unknown words.

What Is the "Secret" to Doing It?

Students must:

- ♦ Think about the topic being discussed and use prior knowledge about the topic.
- ♦ Think what the sound of the first letter of the unknown word is and form their mouths to get ready to say that sound.
- ♦ Make a prediction that begins with the consonant sound and fits the sense of the sentence.

LESSON INTRODUCTION

Say something like:

"Today we will be measuring the thickness of things, and to help you I will read this selection in our big book on things that are thick. But I also want to show you how you can use what you have already learned about consonant sounds and about context to figure out words you may not know. We will use this new strategy when I read you this selection about things that are thick. The secret to doing this is to put together what you have learned before about letter sounds and about using your experience to predict what may happen in a selection."

MODELING THE THINKING

Say something like:

> "Before I start reading our big book on thickness, let me show you how I figure out hard words using both consonant sounds and the sense of the sentence. I'm writing on the board the sentence 'The hat looks pretty on the lady.' (*Read sentence orally and stop at* lady.) Let's pretend that I am reading this sentence and I come to this word [*lady*] and I do not know it. I have to figure it out. First, I look at the first letter in the word and get my mouth ready to say the /l/ sound. Then I think about what I know about hats and who they look pretty on. I know from my own experience that we might say that hats look pretty on girls. But *girls* does not begin with the /l/ sound. So the word can't be *girls*. I think about my experience again and think about who a hat might look pretty on that begins with the sound of /l/. *Lady* begins with the sound of /l/ and hats look pretty on ladies, so the word must be *lady*. I figured it out by using what I know about pretty hats and about the sound of the consonant *l*."

SCAFFOLDED ASSISTANCE

Example 1: Extensive Teacher Help

Say something like:

> "Let's try another one but this time we will do it together. Here's a sentence we can use. (*Write* 'Wash your hands with soap and water' *and, reading it orally, say* 'blank' *for* 'soap.') What would we do if we did not know this word (*point to* soap)? Let's figure it out together. First we need to get our mouths ready to say the sound at the beginning of the word. The unknown word begins with /s/, so what sound will be getting ready to make? Yes, the *s-s-s-s* sound. Then we have to think about what we already know about what is being talked about in the sentence. We have experience with washing our hands, so we need to think about what we already know about washing our hands and what we wash our hands with that begins with the sound of /s/. What could it be?

Yes, 'soap' is probably right. Why? Because it begins with the /s/ sound, and it makes sense in the sentence."

Example 2: Less Teacher Help

Say something like:

> "Now let's try another sentence with a difficult word in it. But this time I'm not going to give you as much help. Here's the sentence. (*Write 'Don't eat candy before dinner' on the blackboard and read it aloud, saying 'blank' for 'candy.'*) If we don't know this word (point to *candy*), how could we figure it out? First, we need to look at what it starts with. Get your mouths ready to say that sound. Then we need to think about what we know from our experience that we shouldn't eat before dinner. I know that I shouldn't eat dessert before dinner, but that doesn't work here because it doesn't begin with /c/. In your experience, what shouldn't you eat before dinner that begins with /c/? Good, the word is *candy*. Tell me how you figured that out."

Example 3: No Teacher Help

Once students demonstrate that they can use both context and phonics together, give them other sentences and have them figure out unknown words and tell how they figured the words out.

APPLICATION IN READING

In this example, students learn the strategy first and then apply it to a real reading situation. In this case, they apply their new strategy when reading the big book selection on thickness. That selection includes sentences such as "Thick is a sandwich in my lunch" and "Thick is the dough when you bake a cake," in which students can use their new strategy to figure out words such as *lunch* and *dough*. Additionally, students should be given opportunities to use this strategy in other text they read on subsequent days.

Adapting This Example to Other Situations

This example is set in a first-grade math situation in which the teacher reads a big book aloud. However, the same strategy can be learned and/or reviewed at other grade levels and in other text material where the students do the reading. For instance, third graders reading Cynthia Rylant's *The Old Woman Who Named Things* (Harcourt Brace, 1996) encounter potentially unknown words such as *hinges*, *chunk*, and *wagging* that can be figured out using context and phonics in combination.

HOW WILL YOU KNOW THE LESSON HAS BEEN SUCCESSFUL?

You will know the lesson has been successful if students, when they encounter new words, end up figuring out the words, and can describe how they did so using a combination of context and phonics.

APPLICATION IN WRITING

It is difficult to apply context and phonics in combination to writing. Writers do not use this strategy when engaged in composing text. However, part of being a good writer is thinking about how to help the reader interpret the text as intended, and to that extent writers should be encouraged to include strong context clues in their text. However, because this is sophisticated and requires abilities that the first graders in this example would not yet have, this application is more appropriate for older students.

Examples for Explaining Fluency

EXAMPLE 22

Quick Recognition of Look-Alike Words

Fluency, whether in oral or silent reading, is "reading like you talk." The single best way to develop fluency is by having students do repeated readings of easy text. In doing so, they learn to say the words quickly and in ways that reflect the meaning.

While comprehension is a major factor in fluency (see Example 23), fluency also requires quick, accurate recognition of words on the page. Miscalling look-alike words causes breaks in fluency. If there are too many breaks, reading no longer "sounds like talk."

Students reading at the second-, third-, or fourth-grade levels sometimes miscall look-alike words, especially the "glue" words in English such as *then* and *when* or *that* and *what*. Even though students have previously learned each of these words as a sight word, they sometimes say another word that looks like it when reading text. They may self-correct the miscue, but too many of these self-corrections can hinder fluency.

Such miscues usually signal a visual discrimination problem. That is, the reader is not examining words for the visual differences that distinguish one from another. The miscue is often a result of not becoming proficient at visually discriminating among visual symbols at the emergent literacy phase of development (see also Example 16).

Quickly recognizing look-alike words is a skill, not a strategy. We want students to do it instantly and automatically; we do not want them taking a lot of time to figure it out.

How Will You Know You Need to Teach Quick Recognition of Look-Alike Words?

The situation: When reading text, students frequently miscall similar-looking words (such as saying *there* for *where* or *then* for *when* or *was* for *saw*).

The data you collect: Note which words are consistently miscalled during reading.

Explaining the Forest as Well as the Trees

Big understandings that you might need to explain when teaching look-alike words:

◆ That meaning getting is the focus of reading.
◆ That what authors write should usually be said in the way the author intended.
◆ That mixing up words makes it difficult to make the text sound "like you talk."
◆ That fluent reading requires knowing virtually all the words at sight.

KEEPING THE MAIN THING THE MAIN THING

This example assumes a group of third-grade readers. They are working on orally reading poetry in fluent, expressive ways for presentation at a local hospital. In previous observations of their reading, it was observed that they frequently mix up words such as *there* and *where*. Today they are going to read "I Met a Man I Could Not See," a poem in John Ciardi's book *I Met a Man* (Houghton Mifflin, 1961). This poem contains the words *where* and *there*.

The Student's Objective

By the end of this lesson you will be able to read a poem and say the look-alike words *where* and *there* quickly and fluently, and you will be able to tell how you distinguished one word from the other.

What Is the "Secret" to Doing It?

Students must:

♦ Note the visual differences that distinguish one look-alike word from another (e.g., to quickly recognize *where* and *there*, the secret is to note the *wh* and the *th* that differentiate one word from the other).

LESSON INTRODUCTION

Say something like:

"I've noticed that you sometimes mix up words that look alike, such as *where* and *there*. It's hard to tell these apart because they look so much alike. By the end of today's lesson, you will be able to quickly say the look-alike words *where* and *there* when you are reading John Ciardi's poem titled 'I Met a Man I Could Not See.' The secret to being able to do this is to look at what makes these words *different*, not what makes them alike. By the end of this lesson, you'll be able to read Ciardi's poem without mixing these words up."

MODELING THE THINKING

Say something like:

> "Before we begin reading, let me show you how I quickly rec-
> ognize these words. The trick to doing this is to look at how the
> words are different, not how the words are alike. So when I come
> up against these words, I say to myself, 'These words look alike
> because they all have *-ere* in them. But the way to tell them apart
> is to look for what is different. If the *-ere* starts with *wh* I know it
> is *where*. If the *-ere* word starts with *th* I know it is *there*. What
> I have to think about is what letters distinguish one word from
> another. When I come to these *-ere* words in my reading I have to
> look quickly at the word to see if it starts with *th* (in which case it
> will be *there*) or with *wh* (in which case it will be *where*)."

SCAFFOLDED ASSISTANCE

Example 1: Extensive Teacher Help

Say something like:

> "I'm going to give you some practice on telling these words apart
> before we read John Ciardi's poem. I have two cards, each with a
> sentence written on it. One sentence has *where* in it and the other
> has *there* in it, with the *wh* and the *th* underlined in red to help
> you tell them apart. I am going to show the cards to you. What I
> want you to do is to look quickly at the sentence, say it, and tell me
> how you knew whether the word was *where* or *there*."

Example 2: Less Teacher Help

Say something like:

> "Now I'm going to show different sentences to you without under-
> lining the *where* or *there* words to help you. You are going to
> have to say the words without that help this time. When I show
> the card, say the sentence quickly, and tell me how you knew the
> word was *there* or *where*."

Example 3: No Teacher Help

Say something like:

> "Now I'm going to make it still harder. I'm going to show you sentence strips, but these are really hard because they have both *where* and *there* in them. When I show you the sentence strip, read the sentence fluently, and then tell me how you knew *there* was *there* and *where* was *where*."

APPLICATION IN READING

This example illustrates how you could teach a skill first and then apply it in a selection. When the students demonstrate both instant recognition of *there* and *where* and can state how they tell the two words apart when they encounter them in print, they then read the Ciardi poem. Ultimately this skill would be applied when students make their presentations at the local hospital. Subsequently the teacher would ensure that the skill is used in other real reading situations.

Adapting This Example to Other Situations

This example assumes a third-grade situation. You would not normally teach this lesson to students reading at less than a second-grade level because they possess relatively few sight words, and reading with intonation and phrasing is still very new to them. Consequently, teachers will teach this skill to first graders only when, in their professional judgment, students have adequate prior experience with both the words and with intonation.

It is not unusual, however, to discover a need to teach this skill in grades above second grade. Even some middle school students miscall look-alike words. In cases where fluency is hampered, this example can be adapted and used. The "secret" remains the same, but text that is appropriate to the students' age should be used.

HOW WILL YOU KNOW THE LESSON HAS BEEN SUCCESSFUL?

During the reading of the poem and in subsequent reading, the students will accurately and quickly recognize the words *where* and *there*.

APPLICATION IN WRITING

The more writing students do using easily confused words, the more likely it is that they will not confuse the words when they encounter them in print. Therefore, students should be encouraged to do frequent writing of connected text in which easily confused words are written and spelled correctly.

EXAMPLE 23

Intonation and Phrasing

Fluency is not speed reading. In speed reading, words are skipped and the reader skims and scans the material as quickly as possible. There is no concern with how it sounds. In contrast, fluent reading, whether oral or silent, is reading of the text with the proper phrasing and intonation. That is, the text is read smoothly and with meaning.

When readers read with intonation and phrasing, they understand what the author was intending to convey, and say it the way the author intended that it be said. In this sense, fluency is not only a matter of knowing the words at sight; it is also a matter of comprehending the material accurately.

This balance between instant word recognition and appropriate phrasing is an important part of becoming a good reader. One seldom learns to enjoy reading until these dual aspects of fluency are experienced.

How Will You Know You Need to Teach Intonation and Phrasing?

The situation: Even though students know all the words in the text at sight, they read in a monotone, or they use inappropriate intonation and phrasing.

The data you collect: In oral reading, ask students to read a selection in the way the author intended for it to be said, or, in silent reading, ask students to describe the feeling the author was conveying.

Explaining the Forest as Well as the Trees

Big understandings you might need to explain when teaching into-nation and phrasing:

- ♦ That fluency requires that each word be read instantly, or at sight.
- ♦ That the author is conveying a message, and that the text should be read as the author would say it.

KEEPING THE MAIN THING THE MAIN THING

This example is set in a fourth grade, and the class is involved in a poetry-writing project. The teacher has been developing the concept of poetry as a form of personal writing by which individuals gain insight into themselves, their thoughts, and their feelings. Students are given the option of sharing their poems with the class.

To aid in developing an understanding of poetry as personal understanding, the teacher has been reading poetry selections from *Salting the Ocean: 100 Poems by Young Poets*, by Naomi Shihab Nye (Greenwillow Books, 2000). She has used these as examples of poetry that develop insights into self while also modeling for students appropriate phrasing and intonation. She now wants to use this background information to help the students read their own poems with intonation and phrasing. While the immediate application is an oral reading situation, she also wants students to use proper phrasing and intonation in their silent reading, especially when reading poetry.

The Student's Objective

By the end of this lesson, you will be able to read your own poems, both orally and silently, in ways that communicate the emotion and feeling you wish to convey, and you will be able to state why you decided to read each one as you did.

What Is the "Secret" to Doing It?

Students must:

- ◆ Know what meaning or feeling is to be conveyed.
- ◆ Emphasize with the voice the words that convey that meaning or feeling.

LESSON INTRODUCTION

Say something like:

"We have been reading a lot of poems from *Salting the Ocean*, in which young poets express strong meaning and feelings, and you have been writing your own poems in which you have been trying to convey personal feelings that have real meaning and feeling for you. In reading the poems in *Salting the Ocean*, I have tried to model for you how good readers read poetry in ways that convey the feeling the author intended. If you have a poem you decide to share with the class, you will also want to read it in a way that conveys the meaning and feeling you intend. So, today I am going to show you how to do this. The secret is to think about what feeling you want to convey and then to emphasize with your voice certain parts so that the meaning you want is conveyed to the listener (or to yourself, if you are reading silently)."

MODELING THE THINKING

Say something like:

"Let me show you how to do this. Let's start with an example like this sentence:

I don't care what you say.

"Depending on the way you say it, this one sentence can convey six different meanings or feelings, like this:

> <u>I</u> don't care what you say.
> I <u>don't</u> care what you say.
> I don't <u>care</u> what you say.
> I don't care <u>what</u> you say.
> I don't care what <u>you</u> say.
> I don't care what you <u>say</u>.

"Is it important which way I say it? Yes, because I convey different meaning when I emphasize different words. Do I mean I don't *care*? Or do I mean that I don't care what *you* say (but I might care what someone else says)? Or do I mean that I don't care what you *say* (but I might care what you think)?

"The secret to knowing how to say it is to think of the situation being described and to then think about what I know about that situation. I decide what words to emphasize according to what my experience tells me about that situation.

"Let's say I am writing a poem about getting up on Monday morning to go to school. I think about how I feel about getting up and going to school on Monday mornings. If I love school and am conveying the meaning that I can't wait to get to school, I read it so that it sounds cheery and bright. But if I hate getting up on Monday morning and going to school, I read it in a much more dreary, dragging kind of voice. Reading your poems fluently means that you not only read all the words but also say those words in ways that communicate the feeling and meaning you want."

SCAFFOLDED ASSISTANCE

Example 1: Extensive Teacher Help

Say something like:

"Let's do an example together. Let's say I had written this poem:

> The cemetery at midnight
> Was dark and shadowy

With ghosts flitting here
And there,
And I was alone.

"If I am going to read this with a voice that conveys an appropriate meaning, I have to first think about what I know about cemeteries at midnight and the feeling that comes with being out there with ghosts. Think about your experiences. How would you feel? Would you read this with a cheery, happy voice? Or with a deeper, mysterious voice? Yes, you would probably want to read it with a deep, mysterious voice, because that is the meaning you want to convey."

Example 2: Less Teacher Help

Say something like:

"Now let's see if you can do one with less help from me. Let's say you were going to read two poems. One is a poem about flowers blooming in the spring and new hope in the world. The other is about the pain and fear of being a soldier in a war. Would you read them both the same way? No, of course not. First you would decide what meaning or feeling you wanted to convey. What feeling do you want to convey in the poem of flowers and new hope? Yes, that's an upbeat feeling, and probably you would read that in a bright and cheery voice if you were trying to convey an upbeat meaning. Is that the same feeling you'd want to convey in the poem about soldiers in war? Probably not. So how might you read that poem to convey a meaning that was appropriate for conveying fear and pain?"

Example 3: No Teacher Help

Say something like:

"Now try to use what you have learned without any help from me. I am going to show you some short poems from *Salting the Ocean*. Read each poem to yourself, decide what meaning you want to convey and how you need to say it to convey that feeling. Then you can read it to us, and tell us how you decided to read it with the intonation and phrasing you used."

APPLICATION IN READING

In this example what was learned will be applied when students share the poems they have written. However, students should be reminded to read with intonation and phrasing in other silent and oral reading situations, as well.

Adapting This Example to Other Situations

This lesson was set in a fourth-grade poetry unit in which students applied what they learned about intonation and phrasing to the poems they had written themselves. However, intonation and phrasing can be learned at any level and applied to a variety of text. For instance, first graders reading Bill Martin Jr.'s *Chicka Chicka Boom Boom* (Scholastic, 1989) can decide what intonation and phrasing would be appropriate when D says, "Whee! I'll beat you to the top of the coconut tree." And seventh graders reading Louis Sachar's *Holes* (Dell Yearling, 1998) can decide what intonation and phrasing would be appropriate when Mr. Sir talks to Stanley on his first day at Camp Green Lake. The example provided here can be adapted and used to explain intonation and phrasing in those situations.

HOW WILL YOU KNOW THE LESSON
HAS BEEN SUCCESSFUL?

You will know the lesson has been successful if, in oral reading, students use intonation and phrasing appropriate to the meaning and feeling in the text or if, in silent reading, students are able to describe the meaning and feeling being conveyed.

APPLICATION IN WRITING

Intonation and phrasing are applicable in writing because writers give readers clues regarding what intonation and phrasing to use. For instance, a writer might say a character "whined," or that the character "screamed," or that the character was "shy." These are clues regarding what intonation and phrasing the reader should use. Encouraging young writers to include such clues when composing their own stories will help them be aware of using similar clues when they are reading text written by others.

APPENDIX

Additional Practical Teaching Resources

Allington, R. L. (2006). *What really matters for struggling readers: Designing research-based programs* (2nd ed.). New York: Pearson/Allyn & Bacon.

Bauman, J. F., & Kame'enui, E. J. (Eds.). (2004). *Vocabulary instruction: Research to practice!* New York: Guilford Press.

Beck, I. L., McKeown, M. G., & Kucan, L. (2008). *Creating robust vocabulary: Frequently asked questions and extended examples.* New York: Guilford Press.

Brock, C., & Raphael, T. (2005). *Windows to language, literacy and culture.* Newark, DE: International Reading Association.

Cunningham, L. (2001). *Phonics they use: Words for reading and writing* (3rd ed.). New York: Longman.

Cunningham, P. M., & Allington, R. L. (2003). *Classrooms that work: They can all read and write* (3rd ed.). New York: Allyn & Bacon.

Fountas, I. C., & Pinnell, G. S. (2006). *Teaching for comprehending and fluency: Thinking, talking, and writing about reading, K–8.* Portsmouth, NH: Heinemann.

Gambrell, L. B., Morrow, L. M., & Pressley, M. (2007). *Best practices in literacy instruction* (3rd ed.). New York: Guilford Press.

Harvey, S., & Goudvis, A. (2007). *Strategies that work: Teaching comprehension to enhance understanding* (2nd ed.). York, ME: Stenhouse.

Johns, J., & Berglund, R. (2006). *Fluency: Strategies and assessments* (3rd ed.). Newark, DE: International Reading Association.

Keene, E., & Zimmerman, S. (2007). *Mosaic of thought: The power of com-*

236

prehension strategy instruction (2nd ed.). Portsmouth, NH: Heinemann.

Miller, D. (2002). *Reading with meaning: Teaching comprehension in the primary grades*. Portland, ME: Stenhouse.

Parkes, B. (2000). *Read it again! Revisiting shared reading*. Portland, ME: Stenhouse.

Portalupi, J., & Fletcher, R. (2001). *Nonfiction craft lessons: Teaching information writing K–8*. Portland, ME: Stenhouse.

Pressley, M. (2006). *Reading instruction that works: The case for balanced teaching* (3rd ed.). New York: Guilford Press.

Reutzel, D. R., & Cooter, R. B. (2005). *The essentials of teaching children to read: What every teacher needs to know*. Upper Saddle River, NJ: Pearson.

Sweet, A. P., & Snow, C. E. (Eds.). (2003). *Rethinking reading comprehension*. New York: Guilford Press.

Taberski, S. (2000). *On solid ground: Strategies for teaching reading K–3*. Portsmouth, NH: Heinemann.

Wilhelm, J. (2001). *Improving comprehension with think-aloud strategies*. New York: Scholastic.

Worthy, J., Broaddus, K., & Ivey, M. G. (2001). *Pathways to independence: Reading, writing, and learning in grades 3–8*. New York: Guilford Press.

Index